The Aquarian Guide to
Native American Mythology

The Aquarian Guide
to Native American
Mythology

Page Bryant
Foreword by Sun Bear

Illustrated by Scott Guynup

The Aquarian Press
An Imprint of HarperCollins*Publishers*

The Aquarian Press
An Imprint of GraftonBooks
A Division of HarperCollins*Publishers*
77-85 Fulham Palace Road,
Hammersmith, London W6 8JB

Published by The Aquarian Press 1991

3 5 7 9 10 8 6 4

A CIP catalogue record for this book
is available from the British Library

ISBN 1-85538-028-5

Printed in Great Britain by
Mackays of Chatham, Kent

Contents

Foreword

I believe the American Indian is the freest, bravest man that has ever lived. The Spanish spoke of the Indians as 'the bronze race that knew how to die.' To my people, freedom is not a political word that is tossed back and forth between Eastern and Western blocks of nations. Freedom is sitting on a horse on a hilltop and smelling the fresh wind in your face. Freedom is looking across a hundred miles of wilderness expanse. Freedom is something that no man can take from you or give to you.

The Indian regarded himself as a keeper and caretaker of the land for future generations. How different from a people who have so rushed to make a profit and pile up ulcers that they have now polluted and wasted the land and do not know whether there are enough natural resources left to last out the next few decades. Valuable resources are being wasted in foolish wars. The air is being polluted and water resources contaminated beyond use. Noise has become a health hazard in many areas. And what of the American Indian? He was an extreme conservationist: he ate what he killed, and he offered prayers before taking plant or animal for food. There are Indian legends telling what happened to people who were bad and wasteful, and what befell the greedy. As one old chief said, 'How come the white man got the country for nothing and now he owes everyone for it?'

Today the survivors of the once numerous tribes who populated the United States are, for the most part, on reservations. Reservations are lands that were set aside for the tribes by the government. (In Canada they are called reserves.) This land was the part the early settlers didn't want. But even these worthless acres have been whittled down, and many of the reservations have gone completely.

The largest tribe is now the Navajo. Their reservation is spread over four western states. They were originally known for their sheep-raising, blankets, rugs and silver smithing. Today the tribe operates a large saw mill, motels, gas leases, oil leases, and recreational areas.

The Sioux are the second largest tribe. They live principally in North and South Dakota and Montana. There is a great need for economic development on their reservations, and on many others. Today the Sioux raise cattle or secure work in surrounding towns. My people, the Chippewa tribe, are the third largest tribe. They live in Michigan, Wisconsin, Minnesota and North Dakota, and the non-treaty Chippewas live in Canada. The Chippewas are well known for their wild rice. They also work at logging and in the timber industry, and on one reservation have a ball-bearing factory. Some work as hunting and fishing guides and go trapping in the winter, while others have gone to the major cities for work.

Indians still retain their culture; in fact, an Indian renaissance is currently taking place. Young people are asking their elders to teach them their ways and the tribes are becoming proud again. You see Indians driving heavy equipment and working in many kinds of jobs, yet many carry their medicine around their necks or wear jewelry to show they are Indians.

So although we now sit upon reservations—55 million acres of what was once our whole land—there is a return of the spirit, a new generation and a new way based on an ancient belief. And the white man is coming to see, that, in some ways, if he is to survive, he must learn from the Indian. He must learn to take better care of the land, reversing all his greedy practices and learning a responsibility towards the Earth Mother, and he must learn that the Earth *is* truly his mother and that he must share it with the winged creatures, with the four-legged ones, and with the fish as well. The hawks and the coyotes and the cougars are not to be killed needlessly. Man must learn that there is beauty and value in a desolate place left just as it is.

Let his greed and arrogance disappear, and let him say, 'The Earth is our Mother.' Then man will come alive again.

Sun Bear

Introduction

American Indians are a large body of humanity composed of many peoples. The blood that courses through their veins is a combination of European, Mongolian, African, and eastern Mediterranean. Anthropologists and archaeologists tell us that the ancestors of the American Indians were immigrants who came from Asia down through what is now the Bering Strait some 35,000 years ago. Traveling in small family groups or bands, the migrants eventually spread out across the vast and pristine wilderness, following the rivers, valleys and canyons and cutting out trails in a never-ending search for food and shelter.

In fact, if there was one reason for the migrations, it was food. During the great Ice Age massive glaciers inched down over northern Europe, causing animals to flee south and eastward. The people followed their food source. As the ice receded, the animals moved east and northward towards Central Asia in the direction of Siberia, and the people followed. Reaching the Bering land bridge, which provided an easy passage, the migrants moved on into North America.

The wandering bands moved first through what is now Alaska and on through Canada. From there they spread throughout the territory of what is now the United States. Pressing on, they went south into Mexico and Central America, and across the Isthmus of Panama. Finally, trekking through the jungles, they came to the southernmost tip of South America. The entire journey took tens of thousands of years and resulted in the aboriginals evolving into a great number of different peoples.

The ancient migrants had diverse cultural, social, spiritual and climatic backgrounds, and their physical characteristics varied. Some were tall, others short. Some had dark brown skin, while others were pale yellow and red. With them came many languages that were expressed in varying dialects and tongues.

The migrants' unceasing quest resulted in their becoming excellent hunters and gatherers. They soon realized that the new-found world was a life-saving paradise. In some instances the travelers settled down, learned to cultivate the land and became farmers, while others continued to hunt and still others became raiders who preyed on both the hunters and farmers, taking whatever they could to survive. For the most part these same lifestyles held true until less than 200 years ago.

The road through history was a rocky one for the American Indians. By the time Columbus arrived in North America, the descendants of the original migrants were occupying most of its vast territory. The people he encountered spoke many languages and tongues, and this became a way to classify them into related groups. (In more modern times this categorization still holds true, with the addition of the way they obtain food: gatherers, hunters or farmers.) There were then roughly a million Indians living in what is now the United States. They were not a united people and had little in common. Some were locked in a struggle amongst themselves for power, land and the best hunting territory, which often resulted in battles between different tribes. To add to this the European invasion brought with it not only disease and displacement, but also more wars over land and food, as well as cultural and religious differences. The changes that resulted were dramatic, and, ultimately, disastrous for the Indians. The whites brought guns, alcohol, fear and pain. When they pushed westward it changed Indian life forever. Many died on both sides. Indian survivors became 'wards of the government' and were herded onto reservations. It was only in the Southwest that Native people were allowed to retain some sense of their traditional culture and religion.

What were these people the Europeans encountered really like? The American Indian was (and still is) a 'conservationist', a caretaker of the Earth. He rarely killed anything he did not eat, and offered prayers before going on the hunt. In harvesting herbs and plants an Indian would never take from the first plant he saw, but, offering a prayer, he would go on to the next, thus ensuring the survival of the species. When the Europeans came, Indians treated them kindly, for it was their philosophy to treat the stranger as the Great Spirit in disguise. Indians brought gifts and taught the newcomers how to farm the land and how they must give back to the earth if they wished to continue to reap from it. The latter, however, was treated as little more than Indian 'superstition'.

Here was a conflict of cultures. The Indian was a man of stone, unchanging, believing that honesty and principle were unchangeable. The white man was a man of metal, malleable and changeable, behaving as if the end justified the means. He spoke 'with a forked tongue', calling the Indians 'brother' to their faces and 'savages' behind their backs. So, when the men of stone came up against the men of metal, the men of stone were defeated. But not without resistance. The Indian loved his people and his Earth Mother, and so, ill-armed and out-numbered, he fought with skill, cunning and courage.

For the last decade, I have lived in the Indian country of Arizona. During that time, I, along with my husband and friends, have spent a lot of time on the three mesas of the Hopi. The drive from our home in Sedona to Hopiland takes us through the ponderosa pine forests of Flagstaff, where the snow-capped summits of the sacred mountains of the Hopi and Navajo stand like mighty sentinels over the north land, on across the high desert country, where ancient volcanic cinder cones dot the desolate landscape, and further, past red rocks shaped aeons ago by the waters of arcane seas. Arriving at the homeland of the Hopi stimulates one's senses immediately with smells of burning cedar and dry desert dust, and sights of small, deteriorating villages, some of which are perched on the edge of cliffs aged by centuries of hot winds and sun fire.

It was a Saturday in June, the time for the Niman, or 'Home' dance, held annually to mark the time the kachinas, or Hopi deities, return to their home in the sacred peaks of the San Francisco mountains. As we entered the village of Hotevilla on Third Mesa, the sound of drums, bells and rattles called out in accompaniment to the unearthly chanting of a chorus of all male voices. Getting closer, we saw the line of costumed dancers, each impersonating a type of kachina. From reading, I was intellectually prepared for what I saw, but nothing could have prepared me for what was there before me at that moment! The sounds, the colors, the smells, the people, the invisible, but profoundly present, power—all this took me, instantly, on a sensual and spiritual journey I had never before imagined or experienced. I knew I had stepped into another time and another world, a world far-removed from my own. On that overcast afternoon, I witnessed a piece of ancient history taking place, as it had for hundreds of years, performed by these people who possess a unique tradition among the Indian tribes of North America.

Since that time I have seen many ceremonial dances at Hopiland, and they have never become commonplace. I have become acquainted with a few Hopi people; I have watched the doll carvers whittle replicas of the kachinas out of cottonwood root, and the potters mold, fire and paint their bowls, plates and vases with sacred designs. I have looked out over the vastness of the desert from the ancient village of Walpi on the bow of First Mesa, and seen a sunset of turquoise, red and gold set the sky ablaze with the masterful handiwork of Tiowa, the Creator. I have watched as the kachinas climb out of the kiva, and listened to their shrill calls and deep chants as they filed into the plaza to bring the legends and myths of the Hopi to life once again. I have gone down into the kiva and seen the Creation Dance reassure the people of their existence and purpose in life. And for all of this I am grateful, from all of this I have learned, through all of this I have touched—ever so fleetingly— another Reality.

Through my association and friendship with Sun Bear, I have met other American Indians from many tribes. I have observed and sometimes participated in ceremonials such as smoking the sacred pipe, and in the cleansing Sweat, and listened to medicine people and Storytellers of the Lakota and Oglala Sioux, Shawnee, Chippewa, Iroquis, Seneca, Santa Clara, Navajo, Cherokee, Wampanoag and Penobscot tribes. These experiences have given me a remarkable sense of 'connection' with the Forces of Nature and aroused my most natural, primitive, instinctual 'Self', which sees all life as sacred. I have listened to Indians speak with the tongue of pain and hatred, and heard others who have come to realize that if their traditional ways and values are to survive, they must be shared with and taught to all peoples of all colors. Both spoke from their hearts, with different reasons and motives.

My purpose in writing this book is to share the American Indian with the reader. I have selected the myths and legends carefully, so as to adequately portray the 'soul' of these diverse people. I seek to bring the reader into closer contact with the brave men and women of the past who fought for their land and people through some of the darkest days of American history, and who triumph in the memory of their descendants, who are the living Indians of today. It is they who must come to merge the joys and pains of the past into some sense of balance, so an uncertain future may unfold to carry the Indians into a new dawn.

The ceremonials I have described are the 'backbone' of an Indian's life, his connection with who he is and with his ancestral past. They are his link with the Otherworld, the Sky Country, Mother Earth, and Mother Corn. These are ceremonies, born from individual dreams and visions, that have served to unite red men and women with the hierarchy of spirits and deities, both good and evil, who guide their earthly affairs. I have brought many of the 'medicine tools' of the Native people to the attention of the reader, not only to inform of their design and use, but to also show how the simplest things in nature can be transformed, by an open human mind, into objects of great and magical power.

Above all, I seek to guide the reader past the veils of misunderstanding about the red men, so that it may be realized that the American Indian is not gone from this world, that the people of the eastern woodlands, of the pueblos of the southwestern deserts, of the Plains and the sacred Black Hills, of the coasts and inlands of the Pacific Northwest, are the 'living legacy' of the hopes, values, and dreams of their forebears. I will introduce you to some men and women of today who struggle to keep alive an age-old tradition amidst a rapidly changing and alien world. I am motivated by a deep desire for those who feel drawn to the ways of the Indian peoples to reach a greater understanding, for it may be that interest that, ultimately, will assure the survival of the 'medicine path', the environmental perspective, and the principles of Indian life.

It must be remembered that our knowledge of the Native Americans has spanned less than 200 years and there is much we are ignorant of. Today's Indians have also lost a lot of their traditions. It is those medicine teachers like Sun Bear, who are willing to inform and share, who will help sustain global interest in the American Indian. From such individuals, we can learn, and what we learn we can incorporate, once again, into society. We can come to know that our relationship with all lives on the planet is carried in our hearts, not, as Sun Bear says, 'written on tablets of stone or in law books.' This truly is the only good law. Perhaps we can come, once again, to take pride in ourselves, our skills and abilities, be proud of our achievements and value human honor. Maybe we can heal the Earth from the pollution and devastation that we have heaped upon her. The American Indian calls us back to the wildernesses, mountains, and seas which would be lesser places without him. Maybe we can regain a sense of responsibility towards one another.

If and when we do, we will live as Indians lived, we will know and possess his values, we will once more live from the heart. What we search for in our 'green' politics, in our search for personal 'vision' and direction, in our quest for honest spiritual expression, in our hunger for right living, in our need for simplicity, and in our sense of justice and relationships with all life forms, Indians possessed. Because of this, their very existence is a legacy to all mankind.

Note Italics in the text denote cross-references.

A

Apache Mountain Spirit Dancers

Absaroka See *Crow.*

Achiyalatopa Achiyalatopa is described by the *Zuni* people as a peculiar being who has knives for a tail. It was he who taught the Zunis the art of sword-swallowing, and his picture can be seen on their sacred altars. All sword-swallowers originally belonged to one of the six Zuni *clans* that are named for the six sacred animals: the badger, snake, *cougar*, wolf, shrew and *bear*. However, through the years, most of these original clans have died out, making this no longer true.

Acoma Pueblo Part of the ruins of the prehistoric people of *Chaco Canyon*, the Acoma *pueblo* is located 60 miles west of Albuquerque, New Mexico. The people who once lived there are believed to have vacated the area due to major climatic changes that resulted in a long and severe drought. Once known as the Blue Sky People, they were farmers who grew beans and melons and also raised turkeys. In addition, they were excellent potters.

The Acoma pueblo was also the site of powerful *ceremonies.* The people believed that ancient supernatural beings had designed the lay-out of the pueblo, which is situated on a rock mesa in high desert country. It is believed that many of their ceremonies had to do with the bringing of rain and were in the form of sacred *dances*.

Adena See *Mound Builders*.

Algonquin The Algonquins were a great people and comprised over a hundred *tribes* that included the Abnakis, Delawares, Mahicans, Mohigans, Narragansetts, *Penobscots*, Pequots, *Shawnees* and Wamp-anoags. They once occupied all of what is now New England, with most of them living in what is now Connecticut, Massachusetts and Rhode Island. They farmed, hunted and fished, and were mainly woodland Indians. Feuding amongst themselves was, no doubt, their fatal weakness.

When the whites came, they welcomed them, yielded their coastal areas to the invaders and moved inland into the forests. They were pushed further westward, however, when more and more whites came, and soon could go no farther, for they ran into their deadly enemies, the *Iroquis*. Confrontations were headlong. It was imposs-ible for the Algonquins to unite to defend themselves against the Iroquis or the English, and they were caught in the middle of the two peoples. Weakened by their own divisions, the Algonquins were driven out. Two years after the Declaration of Independence, the fledgling American nation signed a treaty with the Delawares, one of the most important of the Algonquin tribes, and a Delaware Confederacy controlled most of eastern Pennsylvania and south-eastern New York. Today, the Algonquins are gone from their northwestern homelands, dispersed across the continent.

Alliance of the Six Nations The Alliance of the Six Nations was an alliance composed of six *tribes* of the eastern Indian people: the Mohawks, Oneidas, Senecas, Cayugas, Onondagas and Tuscaroras. The Alliance was formed to ward off the encroachment of the *Iroquois*.

Anasazi The Anasazi, given their current name, which means 'Ancient Ones', by the *Navajo*, were a prehistoric people of the American Southwest, who were alive during the eleventh century AD. Numerous sites scattered throughout the Southwest show *petroglyphs* (ancient rock paintings) that stand in mute evidence of this long-gone race.

It is known that the Anasazi were strongly connected with the skies, for in the great *kiva* of Casa Rinconada in *Chaco Canyon*, New Mexico, there is evidence of sophisticated celestial knowledge. Its circular shape duplicates the sky and its main door opens to celestial north, the fixed spot in the night sky around which all stars seem to revolve. It is also believed that the Anasazi were a people who had many secret societies and followed a definite pattern of *ceremonies* annually. The Ancient Ones lived in *cliff dwellings* and *pueblos* and also built tall stone towers in various sites, although it is unclear what their purpose might have been. (See also *Grand Canyon*.)

Animal Lodge Called Pa-ha-tu, 'Hill in Water Settlement', by the Skidi *Pawnee* Indians of Nebraska, the Animal Lodge was allegedly located on the inside of a bluff and under the water on the south side of the Platte River. Healers, mostly men called 'doctors', came into their powers after going to the Animal Lodge while asleep and in a dream vision.

The wind at the Animal Lodge was very strong. On the bluff a cedar tree, said to be the doorway of the lodge, was filled with all sorts of birds, especially various types of *eagles* and chicken hawks. Tawakiiks, a big fish who lived under the water, would open its mouth and emit *fire*, causing sparks to fly across the water. It is also said that one could hear drumming there.

The animals would sit in council and judge the visionary. Some visions were considered to be terrestrial, others more cosmic in their nature. If the visionary was considered worthy, the animals taught their special powers to the human. Women were occasionally allowed to be 'doctors' if they learned the powers from their husband or after their husband had died.

While most members of the animal kingdom were considered positive in the nature of their power and had the same effect on mankind, there were some who were thought to be negative in their effect, namely *bears*, weasels and moles. The claws of the owl were also considered negative. It is interesting to note that the owl is a rather common omen to many Indian *tribes*, including the *Navajo*, to whom it is the bird of death.

Antelope Chief See *Snake Dance*.

Apache The Apaches of the territory now known as Arizona were a remarkable and colorful people. They were of Athapascan stock, and it is believed that they came from the north around the tenth century AD. The original migrants eventually split into two groups. One became the *Navajo*, who presently occupy the largest reservation in North America, and the other became the Apaches, who separated into several groups or sub-*tribes*, and even further into 'bands'. Tribal solidarity is of great importance to the Apache people and in times of conflict and threat they have indeed stuck together to meet and often conquer their foes. So famous was their reputation as warriors that they were named 'Apaches', meaning 'enemy', by the neighboring *Zunis*.

One of the best known groups of Apaches are the Jicarillos, who once roamed the territory that is now Colorado, New Mexico and Oklahoma. The Jicarillos are divided into two bands: the Olleros, which means 'Mountain People' and the Llaneros or 'Plains People'.

The Mescalero Apaches live in the southeastern part of New Mexico. However, it is in the eastern desert country of Arizona that the San Carlos Reservation, the largest of the Apache domains, is located, along with Fort Apache, which was erected during the Indian wars. On this reservation are found the Chiricahus, the White Mountain Apaches, the San Carlos, Tonto and Mohave bands.

The Apaches were raiders. In the early days they preyed upon other tribes, looting livestock, homes and virtually anything of value, including *food*. Once the whites arrived, they too were raided by roaming bands of Apache marauders. Such raids often ended in death and destruction, for the Apaches resisted incursion by the whites with a vengeance.

Unlike many tribes in the Southwest, Apaches are not *pueblo* people. Instead they lived mostly in lean-to type houses and often in *tipis*, a lifestyle which they learned from the Plains people to the north. In the early days, Apaches were nomadic. The women were once wonderful basketmakers but this skill has largely died out. One prominent basket form that is still produced is called the 'wedding basket'. This container is conical in shape. The rim is dressed with *buckskin* strips which hang all the way around it, and the long strips that hang down are tipped with silver cones that jingle with a delightful noise whenever the basket is lifted or carried.

Over time the Apaches have been strongly influenced by other tribes and various cultures. One of the most profound indications of this influence can be found within the Mescalero band, who learned of the sacred peyote cactus and its ceremonial uses from peoples to the east in what is now Texas. They also adopted the fashions of braiding their hair and beading their buckskins and ceremonial bags from the Plains people, apart from taking up their tipi abodes.

Today the Apaches are involved in several profitable industries that include raising cattle and sheep, other types of farming, and trade. They are also known to be amongst the finest of Indian artists. Their *baskets* and beadwork are a large source of revenue for the tribe, with basketmaking currently enjoying a revival. Known to be expert business people, the Apache tribe also owns and operates a large ski resort in the White Mountains of eastern Arizona. Apaches are also excellent *fire* fighters and are frequently called upon to fight large blazes in various parts of the United States. In recent years they have fought forest fires throughout the Southwest and as far away as Yellowstone, Wyoming and southern California.

Like all Native Americans, Apaches have many *ceremonies* that compose and reflect their spiritual beliefs. The Jicarillos hold an annual feast in early July, and in September the Olleros and the Llaneros hold a reunion ceremony, known as the Sunrise Ceremony, near Horse Lake, which is a puberty ceremony for young girls. Of all the Apache ceremonies, however, it is the *Apache Mountain Spirit Dance* that is the most famous.

The history of the Apaches has produced several men who have become well-known, including *Cochise*, *Mangus Colorado* and *Victorio*. However, none were more acclaimed than the famous leader and *medicine man*, *Geronimo*. He and his followers withstood and evaded cavalry troops for a long time. In the words of *Sun Bear*, taken from his book *Buffalo Hearts*:

> Geronimo was a patriot, a man who fought hard for his people. There were 60 million people in this country when Geronimo was fighting. He didn't expect to defeat the United States, but only to secure desert lands for his people and a just treaty. He belonged to the Mimbreno band of Apache. He was a good hunter and tracker and knew how to survive in the desert. They said of the Apache that they knew every water hole around the country. They knew which would be dry certain times of year. The Apache would carry water using the small intestine of the horse as a container. In warfare he also survived successfully.

Apache Mountain Spirits Dance In this *dance*, performed by the *Apaches*, the dancers represent supernatural beings. Each wears a mysterious black mask that covers the entire head and on top of the *masks* are head-dresses with cut-out symbols on them. The headpieces are called 'crowns', leading to the dance often being called the 'Crown Dance'.

The dance is done at night around a huge bonfire, and the participants make gestures with symbolic sticks that they hold in their hands. The steps are stylized. As the dance goes on young maidens are allowed to join in.

Autumnal Equinox The Autumnal Equinox is 22 September. To the Native American, it was a time of harvest and celebration of the fruitfulness of *Mother Earth*. During this time, *ceremonies* and *dances* are held and prayers said for the continued fertility for all females in all kingdoms of life, including Mother Earth herself.

B

Buffalo

Badlands, South Dakota The Native Americans who live amongst the rocky landscape of the Badlands in South Dakota consider it to be a place of extraordinary sacred power. The land was named by French-Canadian fur trappers and was once home to *elk*, *bears*, wolves and bison. It was in the southern part of the Badlands that the prophet *Wovoka* held his *Ghost Dances*.

Basket Dance One of the most beautiful of all *ceremonies* performed by female societies, the Basket Dance, also known as the Lakone or Lalakonti Ceremony, is a women's ceremony of the *Hopi*. Although the whites call it the Basket Dance, the word actually means 'hail'. Lalakonti is conducted for the purpose of bringing hail and snow so that the ground will be moist and crops will grow well in the spring. The ceremony is performed by women from many different *clans* and is headed by four priestesses whose office is hereditary. Part of the rite is held in the *kiva*, and this involves the making of prayer plumes, an altar and a *sandpainting*, as well as the preparation of costumes and ceremonial smoking.

To make sure that the constellation Orion has reached the right place in the sky for the ceremony, an old woman comes out of the kiva first, followed by a procession of the other women and two men. Chanting accompanies the ritual of the prayer plumes being put in the sacred hole of *emergence*, *Sipapu*, then the party returns to the kiva.

The ceremony also represents an act of thanksgiving for the bountiful harvest from *Mother Earth*. The *dance* is performed by women who form a *circle* while chanting. The *baskets* are held in both hands and are slowly raised to touch one breast and then the other. Next they are lowered to touch the groin. The climax of the ceremony comes with the baskets being thrown into the air while the young men struggle to catch the 'prizes', i.e. both the baskets and the young women themselves.

Baskets Basketmaking was common to almost all of the Indian *tribes* of the Americas. Baskets were used for storing *food*, cooking, carrying and storing water, carrying burdens, heating water with hot rocks and for drinking from. The materials used varied, depending upon the terrain involved, and included reeds, grasses, willow and yucca. The chosen material was interwoven and oftentimes coiled into pocket-like utensils which also varied in size and shape. Most baskets were light in weight but very strong and watertight.

One of the most common shapes was conical, which worked well when slung over the shoulders so that water or other valuables could be carried whenever the bearer needed to descend a cliff or stream, climb, or execute any other maneuver requiring both hands.

After a while the Native people began to decorate their baskets with geometrical designs. Soon these became more complex, and tassels, fringes and even silver cones were added to the baskets. Each tribe had their own unique designs and styles and shapes, ranging from the very small to the massive.

Of all the basketmakers, it is said that the *Hopi* of northern Arizona and the *Papago* of the southern Arizona deserts are the best. This honor would, in the past, have had to go to the *Apaches*, but a great amount of their basket art has been lost. The Hopi do coiled basketry and their designs include geometrical shapes as well as animals, birds, and *kachinas*. The Mescalero Apaches are just now in the process of restoring their basket art, making beautiful pieces out of yucca fiber. The Hopi use the same fiber for their work, along with wicker.

Old baskets are extremely valuable and as a result there has been a growing problem with graverobbing in the Southwest. Illegal artifacts bring a high price on various black markets worldwide.

Beads Before beads were given to the Indians by the Europeans, they would string shells, stones, seeds, animal claws, bones and the talons of birds. Then white men gave the Indians glass beads that were rather large in size and they made ornate necklaces from them.

It was not long before beads became a status symbol for the Native people. It is said that they would oftentimes trade many fur pelts or other valuables for a single bead. Glass beads were also sometimes used for currency. Realizing their value, the whites began to bring beads from the eastern part of the country to the west by oxcart, wagons and *horses*, following wilderness roads and eventually highways and railroads. The craft of beadwork spread from tribe to tribe, and beads were placed on clothing and incorporated into *weavings* and into making designs on *baskets*.

The earliest and smallest variety of beads were called 'seed' beads. Then came 'pony' beads that were made of one color of glass. The name came due to their being taken west on ponies. There was also the 'padre' beads that were cerulean blue and opaque. Varieties of beads grew as the demand grew and beads continued coming to America. Many of the oldest have now become rare and are found only in collections and museums.

Although fine beadwork is widespread among the Indians, there are those who are noteworthy in working this craft. These include the *Shoshones* and the Bannocks of Idaho, the *Apaches*, *Cheyenne* and the *Chippewa* of North Dakota, the Jicarillo and Mescalero Apaches of New Mexico, and the San Carlos and White River Apaches of Arizona. Beading has more recently also become an art indulged in by the *Navajo*. I have seen some beautiful work done by both men and women of that tribe, usually in the form of ear-rings, bola ties, bracelets, *medicine bags*, cigarette lighter covers, and pen and pencil covers. A mandala-type necklace has also become very popular. (See also *Wampum*.)

Bean Dance The Bean Dance is a part of Powamu, the Bean-Planting Ceremony of the *Hopi*. It is an elaborate ceremony that lasts for eight days and celebrates the return of the *kachinas* from the sacred *mountains* back to the Hopi mesas. Every fourth year, during Powamu, the initiation of children into the secret societies takes place. The final part of the eight-day ceremony, the sacred *dance*, takes place inside the *kivas*.

Beans Beans are one of the staple crops of most Native Americans. They are considered sacred to the people of the Southwest, namely the *Hopi*, who have as their first important ritual of the ceremonial year the planting of beans in earthen pots inside the *kiva*, where they are then carefully watered and blessed (see *Bean Dance*). In about a week the beans sprout into leafy plants that symbolize the first lifeform to appear in this phase of creation. Beans are chosen for this ceremony because they grow quickly and all of the plant can be used for *food*.

Bear The bear is greatly respected by many Native American *tribes*. The grizzly, for example, is considered sacred to the Indians of the Pacific Northwest and Alaska, as he is the embodiment of strength and power. To the *Chippewa*, the bear is the Spirit Keeper of the West and is called *Mudjekeewis*.

Bear claws are often worn by Indians who wish to gain the power and protection of the bear as a totem animal.

Bear Butte Bear Butte, sacred mountain to the *Cheyenne* and *Sioux* Indians, rises 1,400 feet from the plains of the *Black Hills* of South Dakota. The mountain was where Sweet Medicine of the Cheyenne received the four sacred arrows from the Creator. These arrows identify the four evils—murder, theft, adultery and incest—and form the foundation of the Cheyenne religion. Bear Butte is also a site where artifacts that date back as much as 10,000 years have been found.

Today the Sioux, Cheyenne, Arapaho and other Indian *tribes* gather at Bear Butte for sacred *ceremonies*.

Bear Heart, Marcelus Marcelus Bear Heart is a Muskogee Indian who trained under two tribal elders and is now a tribal *medicine* chief. He has *Sundanced* with both the northern and southern *Cheyenne* people, and is a respected leader in the Native American Church, a peyote religion.

Bear Mountain Chant Sung only during the winter season of hibernation, the Bear Mountain Chant signals the end of the time of thunderstorms and the time before the spring winds. *Navajo* believe that if this chant is done at any other time the participants will die from snake-bite or lightning. The Bear Mountain Chant gives *shamans* the opportunity to show their magical skills and to observe those of their associates. The chant is said to consist of four *ceremonies*, each of which is different even though they are based upon the same legend involving a family of six Navajo: father, mother, two sons and two daughters.

As the family wandered from place to place, they discovered spring water and the uses of various plants. They also built *hogans* and a sweat house (lodge). The two sons learned from their father how to hunt *deer* and use magic. They were warned never to go hunting south of their home but were given permission to do so in any other direction. However, the elder son, Dsilyi Neyani, decided to go in the forbidden direction, resulting in his being captured by the *Utes*, a neighboring tribe, who threatened his life.

The boy was fortunate, however, for a mysterious old woman, a man wearing the mask of an owl, and one of the *Yei* came to his Bear rescue, and he was able to make a miraculous escape, carrying much treasure with him. This was to prove to be only one incident that involved difficult escapes from harm. Other tales have him rescued by a bush-rat, a whirlwind, a mountain sheep, and the ever-present Yei.

In one of his journeys, the brother came to a hogan where there were four *bears* colored to symbolize the *four directions*, and they taught him how to make sacrificial sticks. He also visited the Great Serpent, the weasels and the lightning, all of whom taught him magic of one form or another.

Another of the elder son's adventures took him to the House of the Butterfly, a place of great beauty with roofs made of light and floors covered with sacred *corn* pollen, filled with rainbows. There he was bathed in a basin made of a white shell, and afterwards he was painted and dressed. The boy continued to visit many magical places, and each time he was taught a special ceremony which he could take back to mankind. Once he was fashioned by the Butterfly Woman into a brilliant likeness of the gods. He also learned the art of *sandpainting*, how to make *feathers dance*, how to swallow swords, how to play with *fire* and not get burned, how to make animals perform magic, and the eerie chant that is now used in the ceremonial dances.

When the boy returned to his people, they had multiplied and turned into a tribe. For four days and nights he told of his journeys, and his people invited friendly Utes, distant Navajo, and many bands of *Apaches* to hear him. Today, the Bear Mountain Chant is still performed and is open to visitors.

Bear Tribe Medicine Society Based on a vision of *Sun Bear*, the *Chippewa medicine man*, the Bear Tribe Medicine Society is a community of non-native peoples dedicated to teaching others to relearn a proper relationship with *Mother Earth*, the *Great Spirit* and all our relations in the mineral, plant, animal and human kingdoms. The Bear Tribe is located on Vision Mountain, about 35 miles east of Spokane, Washington. The tribe has seminars at the Self-Reliance Center and people may come there to learn and share.

Beautyway Beautyway is a *Navajo healing* chant that is sung for aching feet, legs, arms, waist and back, swollen ankles, mental confusion and itching skin.

Beaver Based on *Sun Bear*'s Earth Astrology, the beaver is the totem of people born between 20 April and 20 May.

Sun Bear uses the natural history and attributes of the various totems on the *medicine wheel* so an individual can determine whether there are any specific characteristics that the animal possesses that are qualities within himself or herself—physical capabilities, habitat preferences, seasonal habits and so on. Native people held certain animals in high esteem due to their special relationship with Nature and their particular powers (flight, hibernation, etc.). A perfect example can be seen in their regard for the *eagle* as a representative of the *Great Spirit* because of its capability of flying higher than any other bird, and therefore closer to the Great Spirit.

The beaver is the largest rodent in the United States of America, the second largest in the world. Adult beavers can weigh between 30 and 70 pounds, and they never stop growing. A beaver may be as much as three to four feet long. It has a body amazingly engineered to suit its habits and habitat. While it is a land mammal, it spends a lot of time in the water, and its lungs and cardiovascular system are designed to allow it to store enough oxygen to remain underwater for 15 minutes or more. It has a large, broad, flat, scaly tail, which serves as a rudder when it is swimming and a balancer when it is working on land. Its front paws are very nimble, allowing it to hold and turn a branch it is eating much as we hold corn on the cob, and enabling it to carry mud and leaves necessary for its construction work. Its rear paws are webbed and as long as a ping-pong paddle when extended, giving it its amazing swimming speed and ability. Its brown fur is dense and is kept waterproof by the oil that its musk glands secrete.

Bells Bells are used in *ceremonies* to produce sound and make music. Some *Hopi* dancers wear a *circle* of 'jingle' bells around their ankles. Bells are also used to accompany dancers in other *tribes*.

Beloved Woman Beloved Woman is an important figure among the *Cherokee* people. Acting as a one-woman equivalent to a legal system, she takes all major decisions for the tribe. Her word is law.

Big Black Meteorite Star See *Quarter Stars*.

Big Star Chant The Big Star Chant was a *Navajo* chant sung to stop bad dreams and cure insanity.

Bison See *Buffalo*.

Black Drink See *Osceola*.

Black Elk Hehaka Sapa, better known as Black Elk, was born on the Little Powder Indian Reservation in 1852. He was a Lakota of the Oglala band of the *Sioux* people and, along with several of his brothers and sisters, was a *medicine man*. As a young child, Black Elk saw many battles, some of which have become famous. Two of these were the Battle at Little Bighorn, where General Custer met his fate, and the Battle at Wounded Knee, brought about by the *Ghost Dance* religion.

Black Elk is most remembered for his Great Vision, which came in the summer of his ninth year, when his people were moving slowly towards the Rocky Mountains on a hunt. The child had been hearing voices since the age of five, and oftentimes what the voices would tell him would come to pass. The Great Vision came when the boy was ill. In it he saw the Great Hoop of Life broken and the death of his people. He knew from the vision that his people would lie in the dust for many years but that they would eventually be lifted up once again. He said that the mountain he stood upon in his vision was the sacred Harney Peak in the *Black Hills*, which are sacred to his people.

With the help of his son, Ben Black Elk, the old warrior and holy man told his story to author John G. Neihardt in the 1930s. Neihardt had gone to the Pine Ridge Reservation in search of someone still alive who remembered the so-called 'Messiah-craze' that was born from the Ghost Dance religion. This Messianic dream had come to the Indians at a desperate time in their history, the middle 1880s, and ended with the infamous massacre at Wounded Knee, South Dakota, on 29 December 1890. Neihardt wanted to hear the events from someone who had experienced them first hand, not from those who had only been told of what had occurred. That person turned out to be Black Elk, who sensed the purpose of Neihardt's searching and agreed to tell him of Wounded Knee and to teach him of things of the 'Otherworld' that he knew. The author then felt it to be a sacred obligation to share the things that the old man had taught him.

The book that resulted became *Black Elk Speaks*. It was first printed in 1932, but the general public received it modestly. However the book refused to die, and in 1961 it was reprinted and released in paperback. It was very well received, especially by young people, and soon became a youth classic. The book has since been translated into eight languages and is still in print. In Neihardt's own words: 'The old prophet's wish that I bring his message to the world is actually being fulfilled.'

Black Elk died in the late summer of 1950, an old man living out his last days on the Pine Ridge Reservation and hoping that men would come to know of his vision and understand its profound implications, not just for Native Americans, but for all people. He was truly an incredible man, for his vision knew no boundaries and his wisdom was universal in its scope.

Black Elk, Wallace Wallace Black Elk is the grandson of *Black Elk*, the famous Oglala *medicine man* of the Great Vision. *Grandfather* Wallace is a storyteller, *Sundance*r, healer, pipe carrier and teacher of the sacred tradition to both Indian and non-Indian people worldwide.

Black God The Black God, or Fire God, of the *Navajo* is the being who arranged the constellations in the night sky. Legend says that, carrying a small pouch of fawn skin, he entered the Creation Hogan where the sky and earth lay on the floor. The *Pleiades*, a constellation very special to the Navajo and many other *tribes*, got on his ankle. He stamped his foot and they jumped up to his knee. He slapped his knee and they jumped onto his shoulder. He slapped his shoulder and they jumped onto his temple, where they remained.

Black God proceeded to take his pouch, which was filled with 'star rocks' (quartz *crystals*), and, taking them out one by one, he placed them in the night sky. While he was busy with his work, along came *Coyote*, very curious about what Black God was doing and wanting to get in on the action. But Black God refused, angering Coyote, who snatched the pouch from his hands.

Looking into the pouch, Coyote found that there was only one star rock left. He took it out and placed it in the sky. It is said that this star, the brightest in the sky, is Sirius, known to the Navajo as the 'Coyote Star'. However, it is also said that only the stars placed by the Black God have names, so there is some confusion. Black God, discovering that his bag was now empty, flung the star rock dust into the sky, forming the Milky Way.

Black Hawk Black Hawk belonged to the Sauk tribe. He was a man of keen intelligence and a brave warrior who possessed a strong love of his people. He is remembered in history for the Black Hawk War that was forced on him in 1832. His village was located where Rock Island, Illinois, still stands and was called Saukenuk. During the war of 1812, white settlers moved in and started taking over the Indian lands, even dividing up their fields and possessions. This was done while Black Hawk's band was off on a hunt and, together with other actions, forced him on the warpath. By 1832, 1,500 volunteer militia men were marching against him. Even though Black Hawk tried to get help from other *tribes*, it was to no avail.

The 65-year-old chief surrendered and was sent to prison at Fort Monroe. During his time back east, he was taken before the President of the United States. The old chief was allowed to go to the Sauk and Fox Reservation where he died on 3 October 1838. The white man paid him one more act of disgrace when his grave was dug up and all his bones taken.

Black Hills The Black Hills, located in South Dakota, are considered sacred ground by the Native Americans and are one of their principal historical sites. The landscape is filled with caves, forests, waterfalls, fields and fossil beds.

Black Rock Black Rock is a *sacred site* to the *Zuni* people. It is said that when the ancestors of the Zunis were wandering in search of the middle of the world, the so-called Wood Fraternity was separated from the others and went towards the north, carrying with them two sacred *fetishes*. When they stopped and made cloud symbols with cornmeal, it snowed. Never having seen snow before, the people were astounded! However, they soon realized its value in helping to make the grass and trees grow. They remembered the prayer they had used and that it must only be said in the winter. The Wood Fraternity was accompanied by six animals who are still considered sacred to them: the *bear*, snake, *cougar*, badger, wolf and shrew. When the fraternity stopped at Black Rock, their leader disappeared into a spring, which turned the place into a *sacred site*.

Blackfeet The Blackfeet Indians of the northern Plains got their name from the color of their *moccasins*. It is not clear whether the soles of their footwear were actually painted black or if the color was the result of walking across land that had been blackened by *fire*. They were known to be superior horsemen and once they got firearms it was said they became the most formidable of all foes on the northwestern Plains.

The Blackfeet consisted of three *tribes*: the Piegans, the Bloods, and the Blackfeet proper. All of the tribes were master raiders and the greatest of all the prizes they pursued was *horses*. They were also known to be fearless and ruthless warriors. The white people that encountered them in the earliest days proclaimed them to be the most self-sufficient and contented Indians on the northern Plains. They raised no *food* on their own, but were expert *buffalo* hunters. Before the arrival of guns they ran the buffalo over a cliff to kill them.

Blackfeet people were considered a bit wild and boisterous. They fought their enemies with a great sense of pride and for pure satisfaction, taking scalps for pleasure. They also stole horses and went on raiding forays for the excitement that it brought. They were polygamists and some were known to have as many as seven wives and many children. As a people they made beautiful *buckskin* clothing. They painted buffalo hides with dyes made from plants and created elaborate head-dresses from *feathers*. They also carved *pipes* and stems for their *tobacco* and smoked both for pleasure and for ceremonial purposes.

The Blackfeet traded furs for guns and ammunition with the whites. But when the whites began to do their own trapping, the Blackfeet ambushed them, confiscated their furs, and sold them to

Canadian traders across the border. They came to distrust the whites immensely and wanted them out of their territory for good. But this was not to be so, for the fire power of the whites proved too much for the Indians. It also put a halt to their horse raiding, the last raid taking place in 1836.

The white man also brought disease. Smallpox was particularly devastating to the Blackfeet and by 1870 at least two thirds of the tribe were dead. Yet another blow came with the development of a tanning process for buffalo hide, making it useful as leather. Demands for hides became phenomenal and the extermination of the great herds began, wiping out the food source of the Indians within a period of 12 short years. This resulted in much starvation. In the year 1883 alone, over 600 Piegans starved in Montana and were buried on what is now called Ghost Ridge. The rest surrendered to the whites and were put on a reservation. By this time the westward push of the whites was in full swing.

Today there is a Blackfeet reservation near the Canadian border at Glacier National Park's eastern gateway. Most of the Indians have become Catholic, though some of their old *ceremonies*, for example the *Sun Dance*, are still practiced. The modern Blackfeet are making progress with agriculture and raising cattle.

Blankets Native Americans are expert weavers, and since the earliest of times looms have turned out exquisitely designed blankets, some with geometrical patterns, others depicting animals, birds and other sacred objects.

'Coming to the blanket' is a phrase used to indicate a marriage. Wedding *ceremonies* are often conducted with the bride and groom standing wrapped in one blanket. *Navajo* have a 'wedding blanket' that is used for this purpose and they are among some of the most skilled of all Indian weavers.

Blessingway The Blessingway has been called the 'backbone of *Navajo* religion', for it is a ceremony that depicts the story of the Navajo *emergence* into the present world and the events that followed. It takes place over a period of nine days.

The legends of the Navajo serve the purpose of not only forming the foundation for their complex ceremonials, but also embody the actual history of these people from their own perspective.

Bloods See *Blackfeet*.

Blue-Bird Song Part of the *Navajo* creation legend, the Blue-Bird Song is extremely melodious, much more so than most Indian music. The song is sung at sunrise.

Booger Dance This *dance* takes place in the Great Smoky Mountains and is performed by the Big Cove band of the eastern *Cherokees*. The term 'booger' is the equivalent of 'bogey', ghost, or frightful animal. The purpose of the dance is to indicate the anxieties and fears of the tribe; it is an expression of their insecurities and difficulties in learning to deal with and live in the white man's world. Cherokees feel that the dance helps them to put things into proper perspective and vent their frustrations. The dance consists of four to ten dancers who wear *masks* that represent people far away. Each dancer takes on an obscene name meant to describe the physical appearance of the whites and to indicate, in a negative way, personal hygiene habits, for example 'Pale Face who Pees in the Woods'.

The dancers go to the Indians' houses uninvited, making loud noises and speaking in mock foreign languages. The ghastly masks, painted white, are filled in with bushy mustaches and eyebrows, whiskers, big noses and bald heads. Sometimes the dancers pretend to be sex-starved whites.

Indian women sit out until the dance is over. The masks are strictly off limits to pregnant women, suggesting that the dance is not done totally in jest and that the masks have tremendous power.

Bow and Arrow The bow and arrow was a weapon used by Indians in the hunt and in battle. The kind of *feathers* used in the tail of the arrow added special powers.

Boynton Canyon Boynton Canyon, located in the red rock country around Sedona, Arizona, is a magnificent site. It was once considered sacred to the Yavapai *Apaches* as the home of the Creator, a virtual Garden of Eden.

Brave 'Brave' was the title used to refer to a young Indian warrior. The title 'buck' was also used to mean the same thing.

Bright Star Called Parukati, or 'White Star Woman', by the Skidi *Pawnee* Indians, Bright Star, thought to have been the Evening Star, created all things. She is represented by an ear of *corn*, and the Skidi say that the first human child came to Earth wrapped in a female *buffalo* calfskin, for buffalo and corn were their major *food* sources.

Brown Bear Based on *Sun Bear*'s Earth Astrology, the brown bear is the totem of those born between 23 August and 22 September. The bear is called 'brown' in the western parts of North America, where it is common, and 'black' in the east. It is sometimes also called the cinnamon bear. It is usually four to five feet long, two to three feet high at the shoulder, and weighs two to four hundred pounds. Bears vary in color from blond to all varieties of brown and black, with black ones often having a white or light brown muzzle. They make their dens in holes and caves, beneath fallen trees, and in deserted buildings or by waterfalls. Females tend to line their dens with leaves or grass, while the males do not. They are generally careful and quiet creatures. Brown bears are omnivorous, eating anything that they can get their paws on: grass, seeds, plants, vegetables, nuts, fish, ground squirrels, chipmunks, gophers, carrion and garbage. Their favorite *foods* are honey and berries. Their only enemies are humans and forest *fires*. Bears have a curious and cheerful nature, and they will rarely bother humans. They can stand on two legs and walk for short distances, and are usually able to climb trees better than a human can.

To the Indians, the bear was a special animal. In most legends of the animal world, it was the bear who was the head of the council of the animals because of his fairness, his strength and his courage. In most *tribes* the Bear Clan was either the *medicine*, leadership or defense clan.

Brule See *Sioux*.

Buckskin The word 'buckskin', which is tanned deerskin, brings the Indian world instantly to mind. The hide was prepared for use by both Indians and early settlers by the brain tanning method. This entails rubbing the brain of the *deer* into the fresh skin until the skin is soft and pliable.

Another method of preparation is known as smoke tanning, which involves smoking a hide that has already been brain tanned. The smoke permeates the hide and prevents it from becoming stiff and hard after it has been wet. This is different from rawhide, which is stiff and hard when it is dry.

Buffalo The buffalo or bison once roamed plentifully on the Great Plains of North America. They were a *food* source for many Indian *tribes*, and provided hide that was used as covers for *tipis* and to make clothing, lard that was used for cooking, and sinew for sewing. The buffalo was—and still is—also revered as a totem animal and its skull is often used in a ceremonial manner. In the *Chippewa* tradition, the White Buffalo is the Spirit Keeper of the North, the direction of will, power and strength. The massive herds were wiped out in the late 1880s when it was found that the hide could be used as leather, but today, with government assistance and the interest of some ranchers in the west, they are slowly making a comeback.

Buffalo Dance Many Indian *tribes* hold Buffalo Dances. In the old days these were *dances* that were held to ensure a good hunt and/or to respect the *buffalo* in a sacred way. One example of the latter can be seen with the Buffalo Dance of the *pueblo* people in the Southwest. The *Hopi* have a buffalo *kachina* which dances as a prayer to increase the abundance of that animal. Also the Hopi Buffalo Dance, one of the most popular of the so-called 'social' dances, involves participation by Hopi maidens and young men and is for the fruition of life on Earth.

Bullroarers The bullroarer is a thin feather-shaped piece of wood that gives off a loud humming or roaring sound when whirled in the air by means of an attached string. The wood is usually pine and the string a piece of rawhide cord that makes a noise like the wind. The bullroarer symbolizes thunder and in serious *ceremonies* is used to call in the *Thunder Beings*. Bullroarers are also given as gifts to young boys during certain sacred *dances* and are used in dances throughout the Southwest. The bullroarers of the *Hopi* are painted with *turquoise*-colored paint and decorated with sacred symbols, usually tadpoles, which represent life and the male sperm.

Butterfly Dance This is a special *dance* done by *Hopi* maidens. The dance is currently performed on Mother's Day and is one of the most popular of the 'social' dances. The Butterfly Dance, as the *Buffalo Dance*, celebrates the flowering and fruition of life on the Earth.

C

Hopi Clowns

Cahokia Mounds The Cahokia Mounds are located near St. Louis, Missouri. They are the largest of the earth mounds and are considered to be the site of a prehistoric 'city' and ceremonial arena. There is a primary mound, believed to have been used for sacred *ceremonies*, and 45 smaller mounds.

Cahokia itself is one of the most complex ancient sites ever to be found in North America. It is believed by some to have been home to over a thousand people at one time. The people who lived there were agriculturists.

Calendar Stick The calendar stick was used by ancient Indian people to keep track of the phases of the *sun* and *moon* and to count the days, months and years. Some sticks also had carved symbols that reminded the user of special events that had occurred during the year.

Calumet See *Pipes*.

Canoes A form of boat, the canoe was used by many Indian *tribes*, particularly those that lived in the Great Lakes region, near the sea, and in woodlands. Canoes provided transportation as well as helping in fishing. Some canoes were simply dug out of a large log while others were made from a wooden frame and sealed with birch bark.

Canyon de Chelly Canyon de Chelly, pronounced 'de-shay', is located in northeastern Arizona. It is the site of *Spider Rock*, home to *Spider Woman*, the Creator of the *Navajo*, and Talking God, her helper. The spectacular canyon also is the site of numerous Indian ruins and *cliff dwellings* that date back to the fourth century AD.

Carrington, Colonel Henry See *Red Cloud*.

Cayuga See *Iroquis*.

Ceremonial Lance The lance, for the most part, was both a tool of battle and of *ceremonies*. As a weapon, it was used identically to the lances of the knights of King Arthur, but it was also a ceremonial object that was blessed and was believed to protect the warrior in battle.

Ceremonies A ceremony is a sacred rite that reflects the spiritual views of the Native American people. Some ceremonies are public and some are done in secrecy. The purpose of a ceremony may vary, but most have to do with the people's relationship with Nature. Some ceremonies are celebrations of an aspect of life and/or a deity or spirit.

A ceremony is always done to elicit a specific response. Some are ancient myths and legends re-enacted and are accompanied by the singing of special songs and the chanting of certain prayers. Some ceremonies, though not totally secret, can only be observed by certain members of a tribe. The length of a ceremony can vary from a few minutes to several days. Some are held annually while others more or less often. Almost all ceremonies follow the natural calendar.

Certain ceremonies require abstinence from meat, salt, sex or other human desires and needs, while others require total *fasting*. Ceremonies are often accompanied by sacred *dance*s, sacrifice, smoking rites, purification rites, and prayers.

In the early days there were ceremonies to ensure protection and plentiful game for the hunters. However these are not so prominent in today's society. Most ceremonies amongst the *tribes* of the Southwest have to do with the bringing of rain. There are also rites that have to do with honoring the *sun*, *moon* and stars.

Chaco Canyon Located in New Mexico, Chaco Canyon is a spectacular ruined and haunting site of the ancient *Anasazi* people. The ruins are of 13 towns, and evidence shows that the entire metropolis was carefully planned and laid out, most likely to create a particular terrestrial or even celestial pattern. At one time it is thought that some 20,000 people lived in the canyon and that it was the site of many powerful *ceremonies*. Access to the ruins is difficult and one must travel over some 25 miles of dirt roads to get there.

Changing Woman Changing Woman is the Creator of the *Navajo*, who call her Estsan Atlehi, 'the Mother of All'. In a manner of speaking, Changing Woman is Mother Nature. Her tasks include teaching the cycle of life, the restlessness of the sand as it flies through the air on the wind, the wisdom of the rocks, the phases of the *moon*, birth and dying, the menstrual cycle of young girls, fertility, and sacred songs that help mankind journey through life.

Changing Woman also holds the wisdom of life. It is she who sleeps with the snow in winter and awakens with the flowers in the spring. No one can change the rules ordained by Changing Woman and those who try risk the destruction of all life. (See also *Holy People of the Navajo*.)

Chants Chants and sacred songs are used on certain occasions and for *ceremonies* amongst all *tribes* of Native Americans. Most chants embody a prayer to some spirit for a particular purpose such as the bringing of rain, marriage, or some other social or spiritual event.

Cherokee The Cherokee people were once known as the 'Real People' and the 'Men of Fire'. Today they are split into two major groups: the Western Band that live in Oklahoma, and the Eastern Band in North Carolina.

In the early 1700s Cherokees occupied all of the southwestern Allegheny Mountain region of what is now the state of Virginia, all of the present Carolinas, parts of Tennessee, northern Georgia and northeastern Alabama. For centuries they were a hearty people and formidable foes who were quite self-reliant, industrious and fiercely independent. They were excellent farmers, hunters and fishermen, and also fine artists and skillful traders.

Then American fur traders came through their land and began to encroach on the Cherokee, so they joined forces with the Spaniards from Florida and the French from Louisiana in open warfare against the Americans. The war raged on for some 40 years and the Cherokees lost much of their best land and were ravaged by disease. Smallpox alone cost the Indians over half of their tribe. Eventually, the futility of war realized, they began the long process of adjusting to white civilization. There was intermarriage and the Indians even adopted the practice of slavery—at one time it was said that the Cherokees had over a thousand black slaves. Industries developed and both the whites and the Indians prospered.

Later, in order to ward off the *Iroquois*, the Alliance of the Five Nations was formed, made up of the Mohawks, Oneidas, Senecas, Cayugas, and Onondagas, all eastern *tribes*. The Tuscaroras eventually joined, making the *Alliance of the Six Nations*, but the Cherokee never did, and resisted the tribes of the Alliance, who sought to take over their land. The Cherokee stood like a barrier on the southern flank of the Six Nations, and as a result, the Iroquois never breached their stronghold.

In the early 1800s the Cherokee National Council was founded, with its capital at New Echota, Georgia. There were 33 elected members and one executive leader, *John Ross*. Things went along well until gold was found on Cherokee land in Georgia. This resulted in the government wanting possession of the Indian land. To achieve this, the *Indian Removal Act* was passed in 1830, making it a national policy to remove all Indians beyond the Mississippi River. The Cherokees resisted and sought justice in the courts but failed. An extensive piece of land and five million dollars were offered them in return for agreement to go to the so-called Indian Territory, but they refused.

Armed forces were then sent to round up the Indians and remove them. About a thousand escaped and took refuge in the Great Smoky Mountains, eluding capture, but most of the Cherokee nation did not escape, and some 4,000 were rounded up and removed to Oklahoma, an 800-mile walk that took six months. About a fourth of the Indians died. Today this walk is known as the *Trail of Tears*.

The people in the *mountains* held firm and even though the state of North Carolina stripped them of their rights, namely the right to own land, they remained, and are still there today, forming the Eastern Band. Later some friendly white traders bought land and allowed the Cherokees to buy it from them. The Indians divided the land into five districts, known today as Bird Town, Paint Town, Wolf Town, Yellow Town and Big Cone.

The advent of the Civil War brought more trouble to the Cherokee people. Most of them sided with the South, so when the South lost, the Indians lost too. As a result, the government put John Ross out of office and took away much of the land given to the Cherokees in Indian Territory.

To make matters worse, the state of North Carolina refused to recognize the Cherokees remaining there as a separate nation, and the Supreme Court ruled that their refusal to move would cost them their right to be a part of the larger Cherokee nation. Still they remained steadfast, however, and in 1876 they were finally given the Qualla Reservation, which is composed of one large area of 45,000 acres and several smaller tracts scattered throughout the state of North Carolina.

The Cherokees in Indian Territory later joined with the Choctaws, Chickasaws, Creeks and Seminoles in the Federation of Five Civilized Tribes.

Today the Cherokee Reservation in North Carolina is the largest in the eastern United States. The tribal government is made up of a chief and 12 council members. The Cherokee tribe is one of the most industrious of all the Indian peoples, particularly in arts, crafts and tourism. Each year the Eastern Band perform a drama called 'Unto These Hills', which relates the story of the eastern Cherokee people. The Western Band in Oklahoma also perform an annual drama based on their past which is called 'Trail of Tears'.

Chicken Pulls The Chicken Pull is a game brought by the Spaniards to the Indians of the Southwest along with the horse. It is a contest that tests riding skills and is usually performed either on 24 June, San Juan's Day, a traditional day for celebrating rain, or in connection with some ceremonial. The Chicken Pull takes place on a sandy racetrack where a chicken is buried up to its neck in the soft sand. Individual riders ride past and, leaning out of their saddles, try to pull the chicken out of the ground. It usually takes several tries to pull the fowl free, for it will try to duck and dodge the riders. A sort of free-for-all follows, with all the riders trying to grab the chicken. The winner then uses it to beat off his competitors, and the game ends in the death of the fowl. Most of the tribes that adopted the Chicken Pull gave it some spiritual connotation, usually that of planting, rain, or a blessing for the Earth, represented by the sacrifice of the blood and *feathers* of the chicken.

Chief Star See *Polaris*.

Chippewa The Chippewa people are of *Algonquin* stock and are related to the Indians of New England and to some of the *tribes* of the North Atlantic coast. Today they are the second largest group of Native people in the United States.

Also known as the Ojibway, the Chippewas were once spread over a wide range of territory. They lived northeast of and around both sides of Lake Superior, were also found in the vicinity of Lake Huron, occupied land as far east as what is now New England, and ranged as far north as the Sault Sainte Marie area in what is now the Upper Peninsula of the state of Michigan. By the time of the American Revolution they also occupied the northernmost territory of the timber country that is now Minnesota. This situated them in the middle of two of the most formidable of all tribes, the *Iroquis* in the northeast and the *Sioux* of the Great Plains. When the Iroquois defeated the Algonquins around the time of the American Revolution and began to push westward, the Chippewas stopped them cold. As a result they were considered a strong force to be reckoned with by many other tribes.

The Chippewas were also the strongest of all the enemies of the Sioux and fought them for two centuries. They succeeded in driving the Sioux into the Turtle Mountains of North Dakota, westward into Montana and even into Saskatchewan, Canada. As might be imagined, this process brought many profound changes to the Chippewa people. For many generations they had been canoe Indians, nomadic hunters, fur traders and fishermen. But when they moved westward they forsook their *canoes* for *horses* and adapted the ways of the Plains people, including *buffalo* hunting.

In the early days the Chippewas were masters at using the forests and waterways in their environment. They used birch bark to make *baskets*, utensils and *food* containers and to cover their houses and canoes. They also used it as paper, drawing pictures upon it and inscribing messages. At one time they were trappers, mainly of mink and muskrat. They also harvested wild rice and did beautiful beadwork.

Chippewas were warriors who were quick to fight, making them dangerous adversaries. They battled against other Indian tribes, but rarely fought with the whites, for they did not often encounter them, being out of the mainstream. They joined *Chief Pontiac's* band in the war against the British but the effort failed and Pontiac was killed. Their last conflict was in 1898 when they took on the U.S. Infantry and lost.

Today there are 19 Chippewa reservations scattered from Michigan to South Dakota and to the Canadian border in North Dakota. Six of the major reservations are Turtle Mountain, Red Lake, White Earth and Greater Leech Lake in Minnesota, and Lac du Flambeau and Lac Courte Oreilles in Wisconsin. The customs of the Chippewa are, however, almost gone.

Chipps Family The Chipps are a Lakota *medicine* family with 300 generations of sacred pipe knowledge. One of its members, Charles Chipps, is the spirit interpreter for Grandfather *Wallace Black Elk's Sun Dance*. The Chipps live in South Dakota and may be reached by writing Victoria Chipps, Box 192, Wamblee, South Dakota.

Chumash The Chumash were a tribe indigenous to California. Very little is known about them except that they were one of the first people encountered by the Europeans. Early records of the Spanish explorers say that these people wore skins and had long hair that was tied up in elaborate styles. They lived in settlements, some of which were large. Their houses were semi-circular wooden frames that were covered with grass. By the early 1800s there were just under 2,000 Chumash left. Most of them seem to have fled the invasion of foreigners or died from disease.

Today some 20 Chumash families live on a reservation northwest of Santa Barbara, while Chumash of mixed descent live in many other parts of California. The early people are most remembered for their multicolored rock paintings that decorated the walls of caves and overhangs. The designs consist of geometric patterns, stick figures of animals and people and celestial symbols such as stars, the *sun* and *moon* and even comets.

Circle The circle was sacred to the Indians. It was called the Great Hoop of Life by the *Sioux*. Many dwellings and ceremonial sites were built in a circular design.

Circle of the Chiefs Circle of Chiefs is the name given by the Skidi *Pawnee* Indians to the constellation Corona Borealis. These stars were believed to be a group of celestial chiefs that guided their affairs. The constellation is closely associated with the Chief Star, believed to be *Polaris*.

Clans Clans are *pueblos* that are divided into groups related through the mother. As a rule, intermarriage between clans is prohibited. If the extinction of a clan is threatened, a woman from the failing clan can be introduced to another village, indicating the close association.

Cliff Dwellings Cliff dwellings were common to the ancient *pueblo* peoples. These great communal villages were situated in large caves or openings in the sides of cliffs in the Southwest. Their inhabitants are not known.

The most famous of all cliff dwelling sites is Mesa Verde near Durango, Colorado. This is the location of what archaeologists call the Sun Temple, a giant *kiva* that is believed to have been used for ceremonial purposes. It was left unfinished for unknown reasons.

Cliff dwellings provided both a home and protection from invaders and wild animals for the prehistoric people. It is assumed that ladders were used for getting in and out of the community.

Cloud Swallower The Cloud Swallower is part of the mythology of the southwestern Indians. He was a monster who caused drought and famine.

Clowns See *Hopi*, *Kachina*.

Cochise Cochise was a chief of the Chricahua *Apache*. He was known as a man of keen intelligence and great strength as a warrior. He was called 'The Serpent' by the infantry soldiers of the U.S. Cavalry due to his skills at warfare.

Cochise and his people were at peace with the whites and even allowed them to run their stage-coaches through their territory, protecting them from outlaw bands from other tribal groups. But in 1869, a band of raiders swept down on a ranch and kidnapped a boy who was a Mexican Indian. The raid was reported and Cochise and his people were blamed. Denial did little good. Even though Cochise went to the cavalry in peace, he and his band were taken prisoner, their captors vowing that they would be held until the boy was found.

Although they escaped for a short time the Indians were recaptured. After this, Cochise called his people together and decided that it was time to fight the white men. He first sent his men to run off their *horses*. Both sides took captives but the whites would not negotiate with Cochise either for their release or for settling the problem. The war grew quickly, with much loss of life.

Finally, when a band of Apaches was tragically massacred by whites in 1871, the government made the decision to move Cochise and his people to a reservation. Cochise, however, insisted that they wanted to live in their own country. The general in charge, Gordon Granger, promised him that the Indians would not have to leave, but later he broke his word, and the Apaches once again went on the warpath.

After some time, Cochise called a council with his sub-chiefs, and a peace was agreed upon on the condition that they could remain on their homeland. This wish was granted, and from that time onwards the Apaches and the whites lived in peace.

When Cochise got sick and knew he was dying, he sent for his long-time white friend, Tom Jeffords, to whom he said that he knew that he would die at 10 o'clock the next morning. It was so.

After his death the Indians buried him and rode their horses over his grave, back and forth, so that no white man would ever find the grave and dig him up. (Jeffords knew the location but he kept it to himself.) So Cochise was laid to rest in his own beautiful land that he loved so dearly.

Cohonina See *Grand Canyon*.

Colville See *Tribes*.

Comanche The Comanches lived in the Great Basin and on the Lower Plateau region of what is now Colorado, Utah and Nevada. They were nomads who went about hunting, warring and raiding both Indians and whites alike. One of their most noted leaders was *Quanah Parker*, a half-white, who, in the 1870s, led a war band of Comanches, *Cheyennes* and *Kiowas* against white *buffalo* hunters who had come into their territory. The Comanches are related to the *Shosones* who are found throughout California, Nevada and Utah. These people of the Great Plains were known for their uniquely designed beadwork, which is still done today by what is left of the Comanche people, who now live in Oklahoma.

Coming Out Party The Coming Out Party, so named by the whites, was an ancient puberty ceremony of the *Apaches*. A special *tipi* for the *dance* is built at dawn on the first day. The ceremony is accompanied by elaborate chanting and dancing performed by young girls. Afterwards the special tipi is dismantled.

Copper Woman Copper Woman is a legendary figure sacred to the northwestern Indians. Legend says that before people came she lived alone on the land. She built a house on the sea coast and learned to harvest sea urchins, all kinds of clams and crabs, and the spring salmon. She also ate seal meat and made clothing from the sealskins. But her life was still lonely and she was just getting by.

One day some magic women appeared and taught Copper Woman what she should know so that her life would be better. They also taught her all that humans should know so that their lives could be better. Copper Woman was very sad when these creatures left and she cried bitterly for her loneliness. She cried so hard for so long that her head was drained of all fluid, causing her face to become terribly swollen. Mucus fell from her nose and onto the beach, causing her to be very ashamed. Try as she would, she could not bury the mucus or hide it. The magic women reappeared and told her not to hide it and not to feel shame, but to save and cherish the mucus and to see it as evidence of her own mortality. If she would do this, she was told, her loneliness would disappear. She was also told that the times during which body fluids flow, including the menstrual blood, were sacred—times for prayer and deep thought.

Copper Woman did what she was told. She picked up the mess with a shell and put it with her magic possessions. A few days later, she noticed that the sand in the shell was moving. Upon looking, she saw that there was an 'incomplete thing' that was squirming in the sand. She watched the 'thing' every day and saw that it was growing into something that looked like the neck of a clam. Soon the figure outgrew the shell so she put it in a sea urchin shell, for which it also soon became too large. Next she placed it in a crab shell. As the creature grew, it began to take Copper Woman's hands and did not want to let go. She even let it sleep with her. Soon she began to see that it was growing whiskers like the sea lion, and parts of its chest and belly started to grow soft fur. Its voice became deep and it would scream with jealousy if Copper Woman spent too much time with anything else.

One night the 'mucus boy' left his bed and crept into bed with Copper Woman. He fastened his mouth on her mouth and his hands grasped her breasts. She felt sorry for him because he was such a pitiful collection of so many sea creatures. And he kept her from being lonely. Copper Woman and the mucus boy coupled and she felt full, the lonely feeling almost gone.

Then the mucus boy cried out in a shrill voice like a gull, holding on to Copper Woman and shaking terribly. Copper Woman soothed him and held him close, wondering if her loneliness would ever leave entirely. Many times in the future she would hold him close and they would couple. Copper Woman did come very close to losing her loneliness, but never succeeded completely.

Corn Corn, often called maize, was brought to the Native Americans by the Spaniards. It is the symbol of fruitfulness and productiveness. Corn pollen is frequently used as an offering at *sacred sites* and to spirits during *ceremonies*. Corn is considered by some *tribes* as the embodiment of all life and is called Mother Corn. It is also one of the so-called Three Sisters of the southwestern people, the other 'sisters' being *beans* and squash. Corn kernels are considered by some to bring prosperity, while corn pollen is carried in the individual *medicine bag* for fertility and productivity.

Corn, Blue Blue corn is a unique strain of *corn* planted by the *Hopi* Indians of northeastern Arizona. It is sacred and is used to make *piki*, a bread used in *ceremonies*.

Corn Dance A type of Corn Dance is done by many *tribes* of Native Americans. However the one that is most prominent is that done by the Tewa people of New Mexico. To them it is also known as the Tablita Dance. (Tablitas are thin wooden plaques that are cut out in terraced patterns like rain clouds and painted with stars, *sun*, and *moon* symbols.)

Both men and women *dance* in the Corn Dance. The women dance barefoot and wear a black manta tied at the waist, while the men dress in white kilts over which is tied a tasseled rain sash. A fox skin tied on the back of their belt serves as a reminder of the human's relationship with the animal kingdom and of the days when all living beings had tails. Behind their right knee is attached a turtle shell with *deer* hoof tinkles. A gourd rattle is held in the right hand and is used for creating the sound of rain. A skunk fur is placed over the *moccasins* for protection against evil. A bandaleer is worn over the left shoulder and is decorated with shells of value from the Pacific Ocean. The head is then adorned with parrot *feathers* intermixed with sprigs of evergreen, completing the traditional costume. As with most ceremonies of the southwestern Indians, the Corn Dance is a rain dance.

Corn Mountain Corn Mountain is sacred to the *Zuni* people. Made from buttes sculpted by Nature, the mountain rises about a thousand feet above the plain. This peak plays an extremely important role in the life of the Zunis. They have lived there for many years, and the mountain is dotted with sacred shrines to which they make pilgrimages during certain seasons every year.

Cougar Based on *Sun Bear*'s Earth Astrology, the cougar is the totem of those born between 19 February and 20 March. The cougar is found in the western United States, Florida, Canada and Mexico. Due to their treatment at the hands of man, they inhabit mostly steep canyon country or mountainous terrain. They make their dens in rocky caves, washout holes or thick brush. Of all cats, cougars are considered to be the best climbers. If pursued or hunting, they can climb trees. They are swift runners, although they are not good at lengthy long-distance runs. They are quite territorial and mark their ranges so that other cougars do not intrude.

Cougars are hunters, with *deer* being the mainstay of their diet, although they will eat other small animals. They like the chase of the hunt. When they mate, the female is often the aggressor. She will chase after the male of her choice and then give him a few swats to get his attention. When he reciprocates, they will wrestle for a while before sealing the relationship.

Council of the Gods The Council of the Gods is a group of *Zuni shamans* that appear during the *Shalako Dance.* They include Sayatasha, The Rain God of the North; Hu-tu-tu, The Rain God of the South; two Yamukato, warriors of the East and West, and two whippers, armed with yucca rods, who can represent any two of the six directions. However, they are usually Zenith, which is up and Nadir, down. Their task is to punish any dancers who do not obey the rules of the ceremony and anyone who falls asleep while watching the dance. The Shalako Dance is for the purpose of bringing rain.

Coup Sticks Coup sticks were used by Indian warriors to strike an enemy. It was considered a great honor to 'count coup' on enemies— even more so if the enemy was not wounded at the time. A warrior could also count coup with his *bow* or anything else he chose. A well-equipped warrior carried his coup stick wherever he went. A coup stick is made by wetting wood, bending it, and letting it dry. They were often decorated with paint and *feathers*.

Coyote The coyote is recognized as a totem by many Indian *tribes*. For example, to the *Navajo*, *Chippewa* and others, the coyote is known as the 'trickster', who tricks humans into learning through the use of bizarre behavior. In this capacity, the coyote is *Heyoka*. To the Chippewa, the coyote is also *Shawnodese*, the Spirit Keeper of the South.

Crazy Horse Crazy Horse was the son of a *Sioux* holy man and a great warrior. His name came from a vision where lightning and a spirited horse came to him. He was particularly known for his physical appearance—he had a very light complexion, light curly brown hair and fair features. The whites thought that he was one of them that had been adopted by the Indians.

Creation See *Earth Making*.

Crow The Crows were extraordinary people. Physically, they were tall, lean and handsome, and they were known to be fierce warriors. They were of the Siouan linguistic family and called themselves Absaroka, 'Children of the Long-Beaked Bird'. Other *tribes* called them the 'Bird People' and the whites called them 'Crows'. Over the course of several centuries, the Crows changed from stationary agricultural people who lived on the eastern side of the continent to warrior nomads and hunters of the northern Plains. Like so many others, they were forced out of the east by the *Iroquois*, and first went to the area of the Great Lakes and what is now the Dakotas, before finally settling along the Missouri River.

The migrations changed their lives forever. They almost completely abandoned agriculture and eventually raised only *corn* and squash. Because of their dwellings, their neighbors called them 'The People who Live in Earthen Lodges'. Once they got *horses* they became hunters, fighting other tribes for hunting grounds.

The Crows were split into several factions, of which there were two major bands: the River and Mountain Crows. Both became increasingly militaristic and were led by war chiefs who made all the decisions. They had one major crop: *tobacco*. Smoking rites formed a large part of their spiritual life, and they raised a '*medicine* tobacco' that was used strictly for *ceremonies*, while plain tobacco was smoked for pleasure.

After the Lewis and Clark Expedition, fur trappers started to come into Crow territory. Trading posts sprang up everywhere and the United States government also built three forts but the *Sioux* and their warring allies forced them to close down. The trappers and trading posts had encroached upon Indians' market in furs and other goods, a trade that they depended on for survival, and they viewed the forts as promoting separateness and war.

The government originally awarded the Crow people a reservation of 38.5 million acres of land. However this has now been reduced to less than 9 million acres, for the government has reclaimed most of it, saying the original offer had been too generous.

The Battle of the Little Bighorn was fought on the Crow land and it is now re-enacted every year. The Crows' major ceremony is the *Sun Dance*.

Crow Dog Leonard Crow Dog is a *Sioux medicine man*, the acknowledged medicine man for over 80 *tribes* of Native Americans, and a singer of sacred *chants*. As a small boy, his people gave him the name 'Defends his Medicine'. Born in 1942 on the Rosebud Reservation, he is said to be endowed with great powers. He never attended white school for fear that it would interfere with his training and development as a medicine man.

The first Crow Dog, Leonard's great-grandfather, was a leader in the *Ghost Dance* movement and was killed in the massacre at Wounded Knee in 1890. Leonard was the recognized medicine man at the 1973 government-sponsored siege at Wounded Knee, and in 1974 he was instrumental in initiating a revival of the Ghost Dance. People came from all over the United States, Canada and Mexico to celebrate the event. Crow Dog was subsequently imprisoned for political activities from November 1975 through March 1977.

Today he is a *Sun Dancer* and a *roadman* of the Native American Church, the peyote church. Crow Dog is interested in creating a Pan-Indian faith that will spiritually unite all tribes.

Crystals Crystals have a place in Native American mythology and religious practices. In the legendary First World of the *Hopi*, the people knew no sickness, for no evil had entered into their lives. Due to the nature of mankind, however, this changed and man started getting sick. A *medicine man* could diagnose what was wrong with a person by laying his hands on the body. He could feel the vibrations from each chakra center so that he knew who was strong with life force and who was not. If the person's illness was caused by bad thoughts sent by another person, the medicine man would take a small crystal from his medicine pouch and hold it to the *sun* to awaken it. He would then look through the crystal at the patient's chakras and see the face of the person causing the trouble. The medicine man said that if ordinary persons were to try to use the crystal, they would see nothing. He did not claim that the crystal was magical, only that it served the purpose of focusing the vision of the center which controlled his eyes, which he had developed for this special purpose.

The *Navajo Black God*, whose job it was to place the stars in the night sky, carried a fawn skin pouch that was filled with 'star rocks', i.e. quartz crystals. When placed in the sky, the 'star rocks' were ignited into stars. It is also said that Navajo medicine men use quartz crystals for the purpose of scrying. If a person wants to know the answer to a question—who has stolen something from him, for example—he can go to the medicine man. The *shaman* can focus on a particular bright star and, using the crystal like a lens, can divine the answer to the question. His word is law.

D

Drum

Dance Dance plays an important role in the spiritual life of Indian peoples. As a drama, a dance is usually a pantomimic representation of some major event, spiritual tradition or legend. The dance, as a rule, is a community affair in which everyone takes part in some way—if not by actually dancing, then in the preparations. Some dances are preceded by many days of secret rituals conducted by secret societies within the tribe. There are also dances that take several days to complete, such as the Shalako Dance of the *Zunis*.

All dances are spiritually significant, as well as being entertaining to the audience. Every dance step, costume, decoration and movement has meaning, and it all tells a story.

Dance steps may vary widely, from the slow, rhythmic slide or sway to the fast, prancing stepping that is often subject to rapid tempo changes. Dancing is usually accompanied by music, and the most common musical instruments used by Indians are the flute, drums, bells, and *rattles*. One of the most unique features of Indian dances is the frequent presence of more than one rhythm going on at one time: one created by the musical instruments, another by the chanting or songs, one by the dancers themselves, still another by the clowns or other assistants. Some dancers and singers alter their voices to create certain falsetto sounds while others, though singing in a normal voice, can tighten their torso muscles so as to sing while dancing for hours.

Dances are performed for various purposes, most of which involve the relationship between humans and the *Great Spirit* and/or humans and Nature. For example, almost all the dances in the Southwest are for bringing rain. Regardless of the location, however, dances are held to give thanks for the harvest, protect against evil forces and spirits, honor special people and deities, ensure fertility for crops and tribal increase, ask for help in facing dangers and in the hunt, and to demonstrate skills and physical endurance. Some of the best-known dances are the Snake Dance of the *Hopi*, the War Dance and the *Corn Dance* of the *Sioux*, and the *Apache Mountain Spirits Dance*. Most dances are open to the non-Indian public.

There is a great concern among Native people that their dances be preserved for future generations—if not for their spiritual connotations, at the very least as a wonderful and beautiful art form.

Datura Datura, sometimes called jimson weed, is used for both medicinal and ceremonial purposes by many *tribes* of Indians. It is highly toxic and is never taken internally. It also has hallucinogenic powers. Bronchial spasms can be relaxed by inhaling its smoke.

Death Star See *South Star.*

Deer Based on *Sun Bear*'s Earth Astrology, the deer is the totem of people born between 21 May and 20 June. Deer are sensitive, graceful, fast-moving and alert, and play an important role in the lives of many *tribes* of Indians as a major source of *food*. Many tribes hold sacred deer *dances*, most of which are performed to increase the supply of this game.

Deer live in herds or small groups with others of their own sex, except for the mating season. During this time, bucks are very single-minded in their activities. They do not try to attract a harem, but bound from doe to doe, depending on the interest of the females. Bucks have sets of antlers which they lose every year and then regrow. It is said that they lose them to keep them weak while the fawns are young so they will not bother the does or fawns. They lose their antlers in January or February and do not have a full set back until the mating season in late fall. The deer's predators are *cougars*, *coyotes*, dogs, *bears*, bobcats, forest *fires*, humans—and automobiles.

Degandawidah Degandawidah was a prophet and founder of the *Iroquis League of Six Nations*. Born a Huron, he brought a message of peace and honesty to the Iroquis, seeking to revive the old traditions and to bring unity to the various *tribes*. This formed the basis of the

League of Six Nations. When his own people, the Hurons, would not listen to his pleas, he visited the Onondaga and the Mohawk nations in what is now the state of New York. The people were willing to listen and it was there that he met *Hiawatha*, a man Degandawidah greatly respected, and whom he felt the people should also respect and follow.

Legends say that Degandawidah left the Iroquis soon after the League was formed. He is said to have gotten into a sacred canoe and headed eastward, never to be seen again.

Delaware See *Iroquis, Wampum Bird*.

Dhyani Ywahoo Dhyani Ywahoo is the director of the Sunray Meditation Society in Vermont. She is the lineage holder of the *medicine* traditions of the Anigadoah-Catawba people, and a planetary teacher and guide who has become known worldwide.

Dineh See *Navajo*.

Dog Soldiers Among the Plains Indians there were different groups whose job it was to protect and police the tribe while on the move: the scouts. Outstanding among these were the Dog Soldiers of the *Cheyenne*. Dog Soldiers were 'crack' troops. They were the first to hit Custer and they held him back while the others grouped and prepared for battle. When Custer came upon the Dog Soldiers, he saw the women and old people escaping to safety, and called out, 'Hurry! The Indians are escaping. If you don't hurry there won't be enough Indians left to kill.' Then he got his surprise!

Drum The drum is one of the most important musical instruments used by the Native Americans. Its practical value is to keep the rhythm in sacred rites, usually a *dance*. There are four general types of drums: the hand or hoop drums, large dance drums, barrel-shaped drums and water drums.

The hand drum is a shallow or thin drum that has hide stretched over a narrow wooden frame or hoop that is three inches or less in width. They are sometimes called 'war' or 'chief' drums by the *Chippewa* and Plains people because they were carried by chiefs on war ventures. Some of these drums were painted and were also used as *medicine* drums.

The large dance drums were most common amongst the woodland Indians. This type of drum is a large instrument suspended between supporting poles and resembles a large washtub in shape. They are often called 'pow-wow' or 'everybody's' drums and are usually used during social dances and public gatherings.

Barrel-shaped drums are made from a section of a hollowed-out log that has a rawhide drumhead covering on each end. These drums are used mostly during dances.

The water drum is made from wood or pottery and is watertight. Water is poured into it and a skin stretched over the top. The 'peyote' drum is an example of this type of drum.

The roundness of the drum reflects the wholeness of the cosmos, while the beat of the drum is the pulse of life. The medicine of drums is the medicine of dancing.

Dull Knife Dull Knife, along with Wolf Robe, led the *Cheyennes* hundreds of miles from Oklahoma to try to return to their homeland in southern Montana around the 1840s. Along the way the Indians were faced with fighting off hundreds of infantry troops.

E

Eagle Kachina Doll

Eagle The eagle is the animal most sacred to the Native Americans. Because it flies higher than any other bird, it represents the *Great Spirit*.

Eagle *feathers* are also highly prized and are used in ceremonial costumes, *kachina* doll decoration and head-dresses. It is said that if a person is holding an eagle feather in his hand, he cannot tell a lie. The down of the eagle is representative of the Breath of Life, while the plumage is used in *healing* ceremonials.

To the *Chippewa* people, the eagle is one of the Spirit Keepers of the *Four Directions*: Wabun of the East.

Eagle Chant The Eagle Chant is a *Navajo* 'sing' that is not accompanied by a *dance*. The chant is used as a cure for sores.

Eagle Dance The modern-day Eagle Dance is the residue of a spring rite that is practiced by most of the southwestern *pueblo* peoples. The *dance* dramatizes the relationship between humans and the various sky powers. As a rule, it is open to the public.

Eagle dancers wear elaborate costumes designed to represent the *eagle* and embody its powers. Southwestern Indians consider the eagle to be the conveyor of human aspirations to the Sky Spirits such as the *sun*, *moon* and stars. Participants in the dance are costumed as eagles and the dance itself is designed to simulate flight.

Eagle Kachina The Eagle Kachina, called Kwa or Kwahu, is common to the *Hopi* Indians of Arizona. This *kachina* sometimes appears during the night *ceremonies* in March or in the Bean-Planting Festival in the late winter or early spring (see *Bean Dance*). These particular kachina dolls are not sacred but are created for use as a teaching tool to Hopi children and for sale in the modern art market.

Earth Lodge The earth lodge was a type of dwelling that was common to several Indian *tribes*. It is suitable in places where it is neither rocky nor rainy. One type is dug three or four feet into the earth with two or three feet of wall above the ground. A roof is then added.

Similar dwellings can be built out of sod, like the ones built by the settlers on the prairies where money and material were short. Strips of sod were arranged like bricks to make a house that was warm in winter and cool in summer. Compacted earth also makes blocks suitable for building, but it must be carefully done and the dwelling tested before it can be relied upon to hold up in severe weather. The same is true of adobe blocks. These must be cured for two weeks, and are best used in dry climates.

Earth Making *Cherokees* have a legend that the Earth, floating on the waters like a big island, hangs from four rawhide ropes fastened to the top of the four sacred directions. The ropes are attached to the sky, which is made of *crystal*. They say that when the ropes break the world will fall down and all that is alive will die. It is feared that the white man will cause this to come about.

The Cherokees say that when the Earth was young, water covered everything. All the animals lived in a crowded home up above the rainbow. Needing more space, they sent the Water Beetle to search for room under the water. The Water Beetle brought up a bit of soft mud that magically spread out and turned into the Earth that we are now living on. Then the Earth was attached to the sky with cords.

At first, the Earth was flat and too soft and moist for creatures to live on. Birds were sent down to see if it had hardened but to no avail. Then the animals sent down *Grandfather* Buzzard to check. When he flew over what is now Cherokee territory, he found that the mud was hard enough. The downward flapping of his wings created valleys and the upward flapping made *mountains*. The animals became concerned that if he continued flapping his wings there would be nothing but mountains, so they made him come back. The Cherokees say that this is why there are so many mountains on their land today.

Finally, when the Earth was dry and hard enough, the animals came down. To enable them to see, they pulled down the *sun* from behind the rainbow, made a road and showed him which way to go— from east to west. But even though this brought them light, it was much too hot. When the crawfish stuck his back out of the water, it burned and became bad to eat. To this day, Cherokees will not eat crawfish. So to remedy the situation, the *shaman*s placed the sun higher.

Then the plants were created, and the plants and animals were told to stay awake for seven days and seven nights. Some could not do so and fell asleep. Only the owl and the mountain lion could stay awake, which is why they were given the power to see in the dark so they can hunt. The cedar, pine, holly and laurel trees stayed awake and then were given the gift of not losing their hair (leaves) in the winter. This is why they stay green all the time.

Next a man and his sister were created. The man poked her with a fish and told her to give birth. Seven days later she had a child and after seven more days she had another. Every seven days this went on. The humans multiplied so quickly that the Creator was afraid there would be no room on the Earth. So it was arranged that a woman would have only one child a year. This is so until this day. All this was done by Someone Powerful, the Creator.

Earth Mother The Native Americans believe that the Earth is alive and they think of her as the 'Mother' of all life. In *Sun Bear*'s *Self Reliance Book*, it is stated:

> We must learn to love our Earth Mother and the other beings who dwell with us on her with the emotional force we usually reserve for loving our dearest human friends. When you learn to do this you will transform yourself, and help the transformation of the Earth. Some people are able, naturally, to love the Earth in this manner. Others have to learn how to give themselves the space to do it. It is helpful to find an area that feels really good to you: one in which you feel safe, protected and loved. Go to visit this area whenever your heart tells you to. Always thank the area for giving you such good feelings. Take the area presents of tobacco or corn meal. Pray there. Sing there. Dance there. Feel yourself merging with this part of the Earth Mother. Feel her merging with you. Be patient. Don't resist your feelings. If it is meant to happen, one day you will feel your heart fill with that place. You will yearn to see it, as you once yearned to see a loved one's face. You will know that you've taken the first step in learning to really love Mother Earth, and the rest will come.

The Keresan-speaking pueblos say that the Earth is the center of the universe and that all other planets assist in its survival. The *sun* is 'Father' and the sky is in charge of the Earth's affairs and its people. The Earth and *corn* are both called 'Mother'.

Earth Surface People See *Holy People of the Navajo*.

Eaton, Evelyn See *Mahad'yuni*.

Effigy Mounds National Monument Located outside Marquette, Iowa, the Effigy Mounds National Monument is an incredible mound site, with 191 mounds that are conical or linear in shape, and 29 animal effigies, the largest of which is called the 'Marching Bears' and is an earthworks that contains 10 *bears* in an arc, with three *eagles* close by. Also in the park is The Great Bear Mound. It measures 137 feet in length and is three and a half feet in height.

Elk Based on *Sun Bear*'s Earth Astrology, the elk is the totem of the people born between 22 November and 21 December. The elk is the most regal member of the *deer* family and considered by many people to be the most beautiful. Its antlers, which resemble the branches of a tree, are shed annually. The bull elk can reach a length of nine and a half feet and a height of five feet. He can weigh up to 750 pounds.

Elk live in the woodlands, going to the high country in the summer and coming back to lower lands in the fall and winter, when it is more difficult for them to find the *food* they need. They eat grass, leaves, twigs and bark. For most of the year, elk live in herds of their own gender. They seem to have a good sense of responsibility for each other.

Elk sometimes seem to *dance* together, forming a big *circle*, in which they prance around and sometimes break into a gallop of joy. Elk are fast animals, able to go at 30 miles an hour for short distances. They have few natural enemies. *Cougars*, *bears* or wolves will sometimes succeed in bringing down a calf, or a weak or sick animal, but none of them are a match for a bull in his prime.

They calve in the spring and usually have only one calf at a time. Calves are hidden for the first part of their lives during the times when their mothers go out to browse.

Emergence To the *pueblo* Indians of the Southwest, particularly the *Hopi* and the *Navajo*, the concept of 'emergence' and rebirth pervades every level and aspect of life.

Sipapu, the Hopi place of emergence, is said to be an actual physical place, located at the conjunction of the Colorado and Little Colorado rivers, where the people came out of the Underworld into the Fourth World, that is, the present world.

To the Hopi, all life is a continual cycle which is reflected in the four worlds of their existence. During ceremonials within the *kiva*, the symbolic counterpart to the real Sipapu, Hopi priests and chiefs seek regeneration and communication with the Creator. (See also *Navajo Emergence Myth.*)

Enemy Way Dance Currently a *Navajo* women's *dance*, the Enemy Way Dance was once a purification rite for warriors. However, the dance is now used for cleansing when a member of the tribe has come into contact with a non-Indian person and has become sick as a result.

The dance last for three days. On the third day, the 'black dancers', a form of clowns, perform a Mud Dance, which ends with the sick person being dunked in the mud hole to get rid of the evil that has a hold on them. After the dunking of the patient, the spectators chase after the clowns and dunk them too.

Eskimo Eskimos are a sub-group of the Mongoloid racial stock. They live in a huge area of the Arctic region of North America, the eastern tip of Siberia, and the west coast of Greenland. In Alaska they occupy the coast and adjacent interior areas from Prince William Sound in southeastern Alaska to the Canadian border in the north, including the Aleutian Islands.

Eskimo culture is adapted to the harsh climate and terrain of the tundra. Their *food* consists of fish, walruses, seals, *whales*, caribou, reindeer and sometimes polar *bears*, where they are available. Most Eskimo dwellings are wooden earth-covered houses that are scattered along the sea coast. Only the Central Eskimo of Canada live in *igloos* made of snow or ice.

One of the legends of the Central Eskimo is that of Sedna, the Sea Spirit. They say she was once a beautiful human girl who was attractive to many men who wanted to court her. But Sedna found fault with them all and wanted none of them. Her behavior made her father very angry, for he needed a son-in-law to help him hunt. So he finally demanded that she marry the next young man to appear.

The next day a strange kayak (boat) appeared, bearing a tall young man dressed in furs. A hood covered his head and his face was almost hidden by wooden snow-goggles. Sedna's father dragged her down to meet the stranger, who announced that he had heard of her beauty and had come to make her acquaintance. He told her that he had a house in his country and that if she would marry him, she could sleep on soft bear furs and eat the finest food.

Reluctantly, Sedna agreed and climbed into the kayak to begin her long journey across the icy sea. The young couple talked very little and only the sea and an occasional seabird broke the silence. Finally, a rocky island appeared ahead of them. To Sedna, it seemed bleak and lonely. Nothing grew on the shores and no sound could be heard except for the mournful birds.

When the young man landed the kayak on shore, Sedna was appalled, for when he removed his hood and goggles, he was ugly and squat, his eyes red-rimmed. He had only seemed tall because of the high seat in his boat. Upon seeing him, the young woman burst into hysterical laughter! He took her to what was supposed to be a fine house, but which turned out to be only a pile of twigs and driftwood sitting on a rocky ledge. There were no soft furs. Sedna looked at the young man, and right before her eyes he turned into a black bird. Her husband was really a storm petrel in disguise!

Sedna bitterly regretted her plight, but her father was meanwhile having second thoughts and decided to go in search of his daughter. Upon finding her and realizing her situation, he captured her, hid her in the bottom of his kayak and headed for home.

However, they were followed by the petrel, who swooped down over their kayak, beating his wings and causing the sea to whip into a great storm. Fearing for their lives, the old man offered to give Sedna back to her husband. Screaming with terror, the girl clung to the kayak while her father tried to pry her loose by beating her hands with the paddle. Sedna's frozen fingers broke off, fell into the sea and changed into seals, diving and playing in the waves.

Again when Sedna tried to hold on to the kayak, her father chopped off the second joints of her fingers. They too fell into the sea and turned into the first walrus. With what was left of her bleeding hands, Sedna tried once again to hold onto the kayak. But her father cut off the remaining joints, which took the form of whales. Sedna sank to the bottom of the sea, becoming the Spirit of the Sea and Mother of the Sea Creatures, while the storm petrel circled the kayak in sorrow over the loss of his wife.

Sedna continues to live in the sea, guarding the creatures that were made from her fingers. She has no love for humans because of the deeds of her father. It is said that the wickedness of humans affects her terribly, causing sores on her body and infesting her hair with lice. Because she has no fingers she cannot brush her hair, so it stays tangled and matted. To get back at humans, she calls up great storms to keep men from going out to gather food. During these times, shamans must travel to the bottom of the sea, confess the sins of men and beg Sedna's forgiveness. They must comb her hair so that she will feel better, and release the sea creatures to be taken for food.

Etowah Mound This ancient mound was built by the *Cherokees* and was believed to be used during harvest and spring *ceremonies*. It is now held in esteem as a *sacred site* and is located in Bartow County, Georgia.

Evergreen Dance The Evergreen Dance is the last winter rite of the Rio Grande *pueblos*. It is an important *dance* and is preceded by days of secret rituals in the ceremonial house. Two days prior to the dance, the dancers, most of whom are young boys, go out in search of evergreen boughs. They camp near the pueblo and come in at dawn.

The dance begins at about 10 o'clock in the morning. The dancers, who can number up to 40, are attended by the war captain and his assistants, old men wrapped in *blankets* with evergreen wreaths on their heads. The dancers come out of the ceremonial house and walk to the east where they stand in a line. The leader begins chanting and swaying to the rhythm, with the others following suit until all are moving in unison. Around them, the Koshare, who are like clowns, make funny (and sometimes not so funny) gestures.

The dance ends at sunset with the dancers standing in front of a ceremonial house while the war captain *chants* a long prayer. This is repeated until they have gone to four such houses before retiring into their own ceremonial home. The dance is repeated two days later. It is given to apologize to the *Great Spirit* for whatever wrongs or offenses the people may have done to Him or anyone.

F

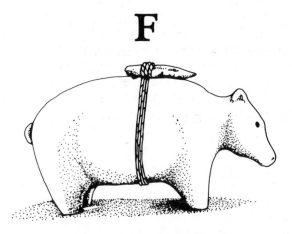

Bear Fetish

Fancy Dance The Fancy Dance grew out of old victory rites and is still practiced today by the modern Plains Indians. The dancers wear elaborate regalia and bright, lavish costumes. Not really a sacred *dance*, the Fancy Dance is mostly for the purpose of showing off individual prowess.

Fariseos See *Matachin Society*.

Fasting The Native Americans fasted for several purposes and at different times during their lives. Refusing *food* and/or water was oftentimes an offering to the *Great Spirit*. Fasting was also undertaken prior to sacred *ceremonies*, a *vision quest*, marriage or a *dance*. It was a way of asking for help from the spirits. It was also done before the receiving of initiation or a special gift.

Feasting Feasting is an important tradition of all *tribes* of Indian people. The sharing of *food* is done for several purposes, including honoring people or spirits, or concluding a sacred *dance* or other type of ceremony. In and of itself, feasting is a ceremony to give thanks to the Creator.

One feast tradition is the preparing of a 'spirit plate'. A portion of each of the foods in the feast and a drink of water is taken out onto the land and is offered to the *four directions*, beginning in the east. The food and water is then left on the land for the spirits. This is an act of giving back to the spirits and of giving thanks.

Feathers Feathers of various kinds are used by Native Americans for ceremonial purposes and for decoration for *bows*, *medicine* poles, *drums*, head-dresses, clothing, *pipes* and *shields*. Particular feathers, such as those from the *eagle*, are held in high esteem, and feathers from one's personal totem are also especially valued.

Most head-dresses and sacred objects are made from turkey feathers or so-called 'legal eagles', which are goose feathers that are dyed to look like those of the eagle. Wing feathers from birds of prey are of special value to Indians for they are believed to hold the power of flight, the power of the hunt, and the skills of sight and hearing that such birds possess.

Fetish Fetishes are native to the *pueblo* people of the Southwest, particularly the *Zuni*. Carved from stones of various types, fetishes are usually of animals and embody (not represent) animal spirits known as totems.

Fetishes are used in *ceremonies*, carried on the person or in *medicine bags* or placed in the home for purposes that include protection, prayers to the animals, and drawing into the self or the home the power inherent in the animal involved.

Fire The Native Americans considered fire to be a Great Being and a sacred spirit. It was often called Grandfather Fire and fire *ceremonies* were one of the first set of rituals performed by humans. Fire cooked meals and heated homes for the Indians and for that they gave thanks. The greatest and most powerful of all fires is that from Grandfather Sun. Most *tribes* had ceremonies, some daily, that honored the *sun* and its life-giving fire force.

Special fires include the one created to heat the sacred rocks before a Sweat Ceremony, called *Inipi* by the *Sioux*. Sweats are practiced by many tribes today and the ceremony is a rite of purification. Natural earth fire, such as that which comes forth from a volcano, is also sacred to the Indian people.

Flicker Based on *Sun Bear*'s Earth Astrology, the flicker is the totem of people born between 21 June and 22 July. It is the most numerous member of the woodpecker family. Flickers are found in a variety of places: woods, farms and even suburbs. Unlike other woodpeckers, they spend quite a bit of time on the ground and will perch upright on limbs as songbirds do. They are drummers, playing their song on dead limbs, tin roofs and wooden houses, sometimes to extract Flute insects and sometimes for the sheer joy of playing. They have several varieties of song, and during mating they put on an especially magnificent display of their musical talents. Flickers eat insects and wild seeds and berries, with an occasional addition of grain and *corn*. They nest in gourd-shaped holes that they dig in a tree trunk.

The flicker is a special bird to many of the Indians in North America. He is considered a courageous bird. Legend says that he has red wings because he went too close to a *fire* set by the Earthquake Spirit to try to put it out, and the flames from it colored his wings and tail red. Flickers are especially valued because of their drumming, their drumbeat representing the beating of the heart and the beat of the earth. Their *feathers* are used in many religious articles and *ceremonies*. Because they are red, they are associated with blood and are often presented to war spirits. Red feathers on prayer sticks are considered suitable war offerings against either human or spiritual enemies. Flicker feathers worn in the hair designate the wearer as a member of a *medicine* society.

Flute Ceremony The Flute Ceremony is native to the *Hopi* people and is held by the Flute Societies. There are two Flute Societies: the Gray and the Blue. The Flute Priests conduct the ceremony, which is performed in August each year.

Before the public part of the ceremony there are several secret days during which a sand altar is constructed in the *kiva* and night songs are sung. The public part of the rite begins at a sacred spring where the priest searches for water to fill three pottery jars that are filled with *fetish*es. Two maidens and a boy represent Hopi ancestral heroes in the ceremony. They are a part of a procession that goes up to the village on the mesa holding the ceremony. When they reach the village the group stops and cloud symbols are drawn on the ground with cornmeal. All through the rites there is singing and the playing of flute music. The entire ceremony takes 16 days.

Food Food is considered a sacred sacrament by the Indians, and to eat is to take in the life force of the plant or animal involved. Food sources are also believed to have a soul and that soul must be honored and never taken in vain. Foods coming from a plant or animal that can be eaten entirely are the most sought after. Nothing is wasted, for waste is a direct affront to the spirits. Before eating, food is blessed in the following general manner: 'Great Spirit, we give thanks for this food and for all the Kingdoms of Life that give away their bodies so that our bodies might be nourished. Ho!'

Fools Crow, Frank Frank Fools Crow was the Ceremonial Chief of the Teton *Sioux*, a healer and tribal leader of his people and the Four nephew of the renowned *Black Elk*. He was born shortly after the infamous massacre at Wounded Knee in 1890, and died in early 1990.

Fools Crow saw life during the earliest days of the reservations when the Sioux were making the extremely difficult adjustment to agricultural life, and fought for the return to the Indian people of the *Black Hills*, sacred land to the Sioux in South Dakota. He saw how alcoholism became a severe problem for his tribe, along with a failing economy and the lack of interest on the part of the Indian youths in carrying on the traditions and customs of their people. Before his death, however, the old leader's hopes began to rise due to the growing number of young Indians who seem to be awakening to the value of their heritage.

Four Corners Four Corners is located in the western United States, where the borders of the states of Arizona, New Mexico, Utah and Colorado come together. It is sacred land to the *Navajo, Utes* and others.

Today a monument with the seals of each of the four states represented stands at Four Corners. One can stand on the monument and put a hand and a foot in all four states at one time.

Four Directions Native Americans greatly honored the Spirits of the Four Directions, the 'guardians' of the earth and sky. They respected them, prayed to them and called upon them for protection before every ceremony. Their dwellings always opened to the east, the direction of new life and all beginnings.

The four directions were always named. To the *Chippewa*, the east is called *Wabun* and its totem is the *eagle*. Wabun represents the spring and its color is yellow. *Shawnodese* is the Spirit Keeper of the South, the place of summer and women. Its totem is the *coyote* and its color is green, indicating growth and fertility. *Mudjekeewis* is the Spirit Keeper of the West, the place of autumn and sunset. Its totem is the *bear* and its power can help one look within for guidance. Its color is blue. *Waboose* is the Spirit Keeper of the North, the place of winter. Its totem is the white *buffalo* and its power is strength and power. Its color is white.

Some *tribes*, such as the *Hopi*, also honor the four semi-cardinal directions and all of them are represented by various colors of *corn*.

G

Sioux Ghost Dance Shirt

Galaxy Fraternity See *Zuni Neweekee.*

Geronimo Geronimo was a great *Apache* warrior who belonged to the Mimbreno band of that tribe. He was honored as a good hunter, tracker and desert survivalist. But due to one unfortunate incident, Geronimo's life was to change forever.

A group of Apaches, made up of women, children and old people, were on a peaceful trading mission. They were camped outside the village of Janos in Chihuahua when the known Indian-hater General Carasco attacked and killed them. Among the dead were Geronimo's wife and children. This drove the warrior to become a man of hatred and vengeance. His heart was dead within him; he trusted no one.

Geronimo killed and fought all across the Apache land, raiding wherever he wished. Finally he and his war band were captured by General Crook, the most successful general of all in fighting the Apaches, and were herded onto a train and sent to Florida, where many of them died.

After being kept in Florida for a number of years, Geronimo and what was left of his band were sent to Fort Sill, Oklahoma, where Geronimo lived until his death. Efforts have been made in the last several years to have his bones returned to Arizona so that they can be buried in his homeland, but so far permission has not been granted.

It must be remembered that Geronimo lived during a time when the white sentiment was that the only good Indian was a dead Indian. This attitude resulted in the old chief being considered a bad renegade by the whites. But to his people he was, and still is, respected and remembered as a brave warrior and patriot.

Ghost Dance Born from a vision of *Wovoka*, a Paiute Indian prophet who some say believed he was a reincarnation of Jesus, the Ghost Dance was performed for the purpose of sparking a renewal of the sanctity and independence of the Indian people. It was particularly popular among the Plains people, and was greatly feared by the whites, for they thought the *dance* signified a reinstitution of hostilities between them and the Indians and that war would start up again. As a result, it was the Ghost Dance that led to the infamous massacre of 300 Indian women, children and old people at Wounded Knee, South Dakota.

During the Ghost Dance, the dancers move in a *circle* with their hands clasped. The dance step is a slow, dragging one, accompanied by rhythmic swings in step with the songs of the Spirit Dance (another term for the Ghost Dance). During the performance, a dancer will fall into a trance, and upon awakening describe his vision of the Spirit World. From then on his particular trance experience is embodied in the dance, becoming part of the ceremony forever. The area where the Ghost Dance was traditionally held was decorated by posts painted red.

The Ghost Dance is still continued today but has not as much significance as it once had.

Ghost Dance Shirt To the Indians who participated and believed in the *Ghost Dance*, the Ghost Dance shirt was supposed to be good *medicine* against the bullets of the white man. The shirts were made of muslin and each was decorated with different sacred symbols and painted to resemble beadwork. Sometimes the cloth was smoked to give it a color like *buckskin* and upon first glance one would not know that the shirts were not actually made of hide.

However, as protection from bullets, the Ghost Dance shirts did not work. Most of the *Sioux* who lost their lives in the massacre at Wounded Knee in December of 1890 were wearing them in vain.

Ghost Wife This is a legend of the Brule *Sioux* and was told by *Leonard Crow Dog* in 1968.

There was once a man who was a good hunter and provider for his family, which consisted of a pregnant wife and two small children. But during a difficult birth no amount of sacred *medicine* could save his wife, and she died.

Sometime after her death, the husband was walking near his *tipi* when he saw a ghost. It appeared like a white fog and was shaped like a woman. He knew it was his wife. She told him that she knew of his grief and that she could arrange for him and the children to join her so that they could walk the *Milky Way* together and never be separated again.

The husband invited the ghost into the tipi so they could talk. He told her that he was not ready to die and that the children were too young to die. He said that she should find a way to return to life and join them again. She replied that she did not know if she could but that she would return in four days with an answer.

Four days later, the wife returned and told her husband that it had been arranged for her to come back to life. He was told to make a curtain of *buffalo* hides for her to hide behind, and also that he was not to look at her or touch her for four days or she would remain dead.

The husband followed every instruction and the wife came back to life. The family lived happily together as if she had never died, then, years later, the man fell in love with another woman. He told his wife that he was going to take a second spouse who would help her with the work and give her company when he was on the hunt. But things did not go well, for even though the first wife tried to get along with the second wife, the second wife was argumentative and jealous. The new wife accused the old wife of being nothing but a ghost and tried to chase her back to the Milky Way. As a result, the first wife disappeared, taking her husband and children with her, all of them vanishing without a trace! Then the second wife was sorry for what she had said but that did not bring them back.

Giant Medicine Society One of the four *medicine* societies of the *pueblo* people of the Southwest, the Giant Medicine Society ensures the well-being of the people by exorcising disease through sacred *chants*. Most popular with the people of the *Zia* pueblo of New Mexico, it is believed that the power to heal is given to the priests by supernatural animals. That power, in turn, resides in the *fetishes*.

The Giant Medicine Society does its work in the sacred *kiva*. The priests sit behind a line of fetishes that embody the sacred animal spirits and a line of cornmeal that separates them from the sick person. The *shamans* hold plumes and straws in one hand and a rattle in the other. The sick person sits on the floor of the kiva in front of the shamans, behind the line of cornmeal, while *healing* prayers and chants are conducted on their behalf. The line of cornmeal is believed to set up a sort of 'psychic barrier' to protect the medicine workers from the illnesses involved with their patients.

Gitche Manitou Gitche Manitou is the *Chippewa* name for the *Great Spirit*.

Giveaway The Giveaway is an act of giving *food*, clothing, sacred objects, and other valuables. Oftentimes a person who knows or feels that death is near will call together family and friends and give away all or most personal belongings. Giveaways are also held after many *ceremonies* and on some social occasions.

Glooscap Glooscap was the first man to many Algonquian *tribes* such as the Passamaquoddy of Maine. Legend says that he conquered a race of giants and magicians, cunning sorcerers, a wicked spirit of the night and a host of goblins and fiends. After this, he felt proud and boasted to a woman that he had conquered all that there was to conquer. She informed him that he had not, for there was still one left to overcome—Wasis had not been conquered.

Glooscap knew Wasis to be only a baby! But when he beckoned the child to come to him, Wasis refused. So Glooscap turned himself into a songbird to get the child's attention. It did not work. Glooscap went into a rage and ordered the child to come to him at once. Still Wasis refused, screaming with irritation.

Next Glooscap called up all his magical power and recited the most potent spells and sang the most terrible songs he knew. But Wasis only smiled and looked bored. Himself conquered, Glooscap left the house in despair, while the child cried 'Goo, goo!' Indians say that when a baby makes this sound, it is remembering the time it conquered Glooscap.

Gluscap Gluscap is a legendary hero of the Micmac Indians, who say he came to the shores of the Earth in a stone *canoe* which turned into an island that still remains off the coast of Nova Scotia. His *bow* was made of stone and he possessed great strength. He shot his arrows into the trees and the people evolved from the bark.

Gluscap had a brother named Malsum, who had come to the world with him but was constantly opposing him. Malsum made the poisonous plants and gave the animals teeth and claws so they could fight being killed for *food*. He was friends with all of the forces and beings of the darkness.

The Micmacs believe that the world is a better place because Gluscap came and the battles between Gluscap and Malsum show the constant war between good and evil.

Good Red Road The good red road or path is a term used by the Plains people. When one is walking the good red road, one is living right and following the rules of the Creator.

Gourds Gourds are the fruit of various plants in the cucumber and melon families which harden when dried. The Indians used gourds to make bowls, dippers and *rattles*. Gourds used as rattles are filled with pebbles, shells, *beads*, dried *beans* or sand to make a noise for keeping rhythm to the sacred songs or music. When used for ceremonial purposes, as in special ceremonial bowls and rattles, they are usually brightly painted with geometric patterns or sacred images. These designs often indicate what ceremony the object is to be used for.

Grand Canyon The Grand Canyon is acclaimed as one of the most awe-inspiring natural spectacles on *Mother Earth*. One of the seven natural wonders of the world, it has been named a World Heritage Site because of its natural and cultural features, which are considered to have universal value to all humankind. The canyon winds in a generally east-to-west direction across nearly 278 miles of northern Arizona. Its width ranges from a mile to 18 miles and it is more than a mile deep in some places.

The Grand Canyon is a *sacred site* to many of the Southwestern Indian *tribes*, particularly the *Hopi*, Paiutes, Hualapais, and the *Havasupais*—the latter actually being residents on part of the canyon's floor. For the Hopi, it is the site of *Sipapu*, the place of *emergence*, which is located at the confluence of the Colorado and Little Colorado rivers.

Prehistoric Indians were the Grand Canyon's first inhabitants, arriving there some 11,000 years ago. Then the *Anasazi*, whose name means 'Ancient Ones', came into the eastern canyon about 1,500 years ago, about the same time as the Cohonina migrated into the western section. More than 2,000 Anasazi sites have been found at the canyon. These people raised *corn*, *beans* and squash, and were also hunters and gatherers. They traded with their western neighbors, the Cohonina, who were also agriculturalists. They also made pottery and *baskets* and painted and carved images, now known as *petroglyphs*, on rocks. The Anasazi abandoned the canyon some 800 years ago, presumably due to a severe and prolonged drought, migrated to the east and became the ancestors of today's Hopis. The Cohonina left the canyon at the same time and may have joined their eastward migrations. As with several tribes of Native Americans, particularly in the Southwest, they then disappeared without trace.

Some 150 years later the Hualapais and the Havasupais came into the canyon and are still there today. The *Navajo*, the last of the Indians to come to the Grand Canyon, arrived about 600 years ago. Their reservation borders the eastern side of the canyon.

Grandmother/Grandfather Grandmother and Grandfather are terms used by Indian people to show respect for an elder, whether that elder is a blood relation or not. Grandfather is also a term used by the *Sioux* for *Wankan-Tanka*, the *Great Spirit*. The sacred Grandmothers and Grandfathers indicate any special spirit forces or deities of many *tribes*.

Grass Dance Performed by the Flathead Indians of Montana, the Grass Dance was a victory *dance* held to celebrate success in battle. At one time it mistakenly became known as a war dance.

The Grass Dance originated with the Omaha Indians, and was first called the Omaha Dance. The dancers wore grass bustles to signify the grassy plains of their homeland and head-dresses made of *deer* tail, which is called a 'roach'. Roaches are still common to some *tribes* and dances.

Great Cleansing Ceremony Performed by the Skidi band of the *Pawnee* Indians of Nebraska, the Great Cleansing Ceremony was held prior to a hunt. The ceremony embodied all the beliefs and spiritual practices of the Skidi.

During the rite, the people would carry all sacred objects to a stream and wash them symbolically. Then they would clean the entire village before washing themselves. The ceremony took place under the direction of the Big Black Meteorite Medicine Bundle, who was the master of general ceremonial procedures and the patron of knowledge of the Earth, doctors, and the waters, and was the controller of the night and animals, especially the *buffalo*. The Great Cleansing was held twice a year.

Great Spirit Great Spirit is the name given to the all-pervading force of the Creator that dwells in all living things. Most *tribes* had a translation of this term in their own *language*. Such examples are the *Gitche Manitou* of the *Chippewa*, *Taiowa* of the *Hopi* and *Wankan-Tanka* of the *Sioux*.

Great Star Great Star, the male Morning Star, was believed by the Skidi *Pawnee* of Nebraska to have been the first object placed in the heavens by the Creator, *Tirawahat*. Great Star is the Chief Warrior of all stars, giving warriors their power and helping them to be successful in battle. He is also the strongest power in the *Milky Way*, the most potent of all stars and ruler over all minor stars. Being stationed in the east, he has special powers to drive the Sky People (stars) westwards, making sure that none lags behind.

Great Star is symbolized by the hawk, who kills with his wings, and the color associated with him is red, representing *fire*. His task is to replenish the fires of the *sun*. The Skidi say that the Great Star originated from a Ta-hu-ru (meteor) and that to carry a piece of meteorite in one's *medicine* bundle or in one's *moccasins* was 'good medicine' and was quite common.

Great Star demanded human sacrifice because of his trials of fathering the human race. This was done every three to five years and usually involved the ceremonial killing of a young maiden.

Green Corn Dance A ceremony to acknowledge a new year, the Green Corn Dance is common to most *tribes* of Native Americans, and is a celebration of the first *corn* crop of the season.

To begin the ceremony a special *fire* is built with the logs laid out in the *four directions*, then the sacred Grandfather Spirits are welcomed.

This is also a time when the people make prayers to rid the tribe of negativity and sickness so they can go to the ceremony cleansed. Marriages are also solemnized and the people allowed to put on new ceremonial outfits for the first time.

Grey Antelope Grey Antelope is a *Tewa pueblo medicine man*, a healer, chanter and dancer. He has danced with the Humbios Clan Dancers, an inter-racial *dance* group, who have performed the sacred Buffalo, Eagle, Bow, and *Corn Dances*. Grey Antelope has also been a frequent teacher at *Sun Bear*'s Medicine Wheel Gatherings for the last decade.

H

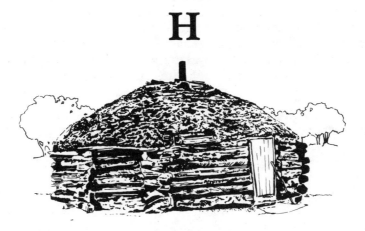

Navajo Hogan

Hako Ceremony Hako is a *Pawnee* ceremony that is usually held in the spring— although it has no fixed time—to ensure peace and friendship and to pray for the gifts of long life, strength and prosperity.

During the ceremony, there is a ritual exchange of gifts between the *clans* and the peace pipe is smoked (see *Pipes*). The ceremony requires two groups of participants: the Father Group and the Children Group. At the end, the two groups merge into one. Hako is also a ceremony that offers a prayer for children so that the tribe will increase and be strong and so the people will live long and happy lives.

Hanblecheyapi Hanblecheyapi is a sacred ceremony of the *Sioux* Indians and is commonly known as 'Crying for a Vision'. Today it is usually referred to as a *Vision Quest*.

Handsome Lake Handsome Lake was a Seneca chief and a visionary prophet. An abuser of alcohol, he once fell into a drunken unconscious state during which he had a vision of angels who appeared to him and gave him guidance, particularly as to how he could rid himself and others of the curse of alcohol. After this, he encouraged his people to turn back to the *Iroquis* religion started by *Degandawidah*, and revised much of it, adding Christian elements. It is said that his preaching on the subject was so inspiring that hundreds of Iroquis were convinced to follow the new version of their religion he had started. This brought him into conflict with the traditionalists among his people, whose secret societies Handsome Lake tried to banish. He also tried to tell the people that they should track down Indians who were witches and get rid of them, even if they had to kill them.

In spite of the conflict, however, there can be no doubt that Handsome Lake helped to give the Iroquis back their sense of pride and helped in the eventual regeneration of the best of their culture.

Happy Hunting Ground This term was used by some Indian *tribes* to denote 'heaven' or the 'spirit world', which was a land with an abundance of game, hence the name.

Harrison, William Henry See *Tecumseh*.

Harvest Ceremonies Most Indian *tribes* held a harvest ceremony of some kind, particularly the agriculturists. Some of the most significant were the three *ceremonies* performed annually by the Skidi *Pawnee* of Nebraska. These were the Green Corn, Mature Harvest and Four-Pole ceremonies.

The Green Corn Ceremony was held under the Evening Star for the purpose of renewing the Evening Star Medicine Bundle's powers for the coming year. There were no songs or *dances* during this rite.

The Mature Harvest Ceremony was held during the *corn* gathering. It was the major harvest rite and was held under the authority of the four semi-cardinal directions.

The Four-Pole Ceremony was held under the auspices of the power of the Skull Medicine Bundle of the Wonderful Person and signified a celebration of the world and life. During this rite, the warriors went out in each of the *four directions* to see that their land was safe.

Havasupai Known as the 'People of the Blue Waters', the Havasupai are the only Indian tribe that live within the boundaries of a national park, the *Grand Canyon* in Arizona. Their reservation includes the Havasu Canyon, which extends south from the Colorado River. Their village, called Supai, is very isolated and there are no roads, only hiking trails, leading to it. They are expert basketmakers.

A dying culture, these Indian people have a legend that concerns a spire of rocks that looms above their village. It is said that when the rocks crumble and fall their culture will come to an end.

Healing Native Americans have wonderful healing knowledge and powers. Healing is done through the use of herbs, *sandpaintings* (on the part of the *Navajo*), chanting, prayer, purification *ceremonies* and sacred songs. The healer of a tribe is generally referred to as the *medicine man* or woman. The following is a story of how healing came to the *Chippewa* people.

Once an old man who had great sores on his body came to a Chippewa village. He was very hungry and tired. A woman saw him and invited him into her lodge. He accepted and she sat him down and fed him. Seeing her concern for his sores, the old man told her to go and fetch certain herbs and wash the sores with them. She did so and he was healed.

Then the old man became sick again. Once more he told the woman to go and get certain plants. She obeyed, and once more he was healed. This went on for some time, and the woman was taught how to heal virtually every illness with the plants. She came to realize that her visitor was a 'Spirit Man' who had come to teach healing to her people.

The healing clan of the Chippewa is the Bear Clan (see also *bear*).

The White Mountain *Apache* people also have a story about how the healing ceremonies came to them. They say that when the Earth was made, the Creator planned for each person to have a piece of land to live upon. The Apaches had their place but they did not like it, and asked permission from the Creator to move. Permission was granted and that made the people very happy.

Then two among them took sick, and the people were baffled, for they neither knew of illness nor how to cure it. There happened to be four men standing there, one in each direction. The Creator spoke to them and told them that curing knowledge was available. So after four nights of sacred praying and chanting, the four men went to the sick people and said some words over them and they were healed. Since that time, the Apache have had curing ceremonies and knowledge of different kinds of illness.

Heyoka Clowns exist in almost all Indian cultures in North America, and the Heyoka is a Dakota clown. He reverses his behavior by speaking contrarily and riding his horse backwards. In fact everything he does is opposite to what is considered normal behavior.

Although the Heyoka can be amusing, he is given tremendous respect. Indians are keenly aware of contradictions and they consider them fundamental to life itself. They also feel that the extraordinary is awesome; perversity a significant quality and not something to be feared or ridiculed, for it is truly knowledge of another, higher, reality.

The *Sioux* believe that the Heyoka has been given the greatest possible vision—that of a *Thunder Being*. It is said that the Thunder Being wears the Heyoka around his neck as a human would wear a necklace or sacred object.

Hiawatha Not to be confused with Longfellow's hero, Hiawatha was a Mohawk Indian who, along with the Huron *Degandawidah*, helped to form the original Five Nations Confederacy of the *Iroquis*. The league became a six-nation one when the Tuscaroras joined with the Seneca, Mohawks, Oneidas, Onondagas and Cayugas.

Hiawatha was convinced that Degandawidah was a sacred Being and that the Indians should listen to what he was telling them about the right way to live. Hiawatha himself had led an evil life after his wife and children had been murdered by an Onondagan Indian, but changed his ways when he met Degandawidah.

Hogan Hogans are *Navajo* dwellings that are modeled after their concept of the world. They are eight-sided houses shaped like the sky. Inside, the posts are symbolic of the sacred directions. People move around within the hogan in a sunwise direction.

Holy People of the Navajo The Holy People of the Navajo came from beneath the Earth, being pushed upward by a flood until they reached the present world. It was they who created the Earth Surface People, ancestors of the *Navajo*, and taught them how to live and control the forces of Nature.

Changing Woman is the most prominent of the Holy People. She and her husband, the *sun*, had twin sons who were fine warriors, named Monster Slayer and Born of Water. They slew all the monsters who threatened the Earth.

The Holy People, for the most part, are friendly to humans. Other Holy People are Water Sprinkler, who brings rain, and *Spider Woman*, who taught the people *weaving*.

Hoop Dance Although the origins of the Hoop Dance are unknown, it is one of the most colorful and popular *dance*s of the Southwestern Indians, mainly the *Navajo*. It is thought that the Hoop Dance may be a reenactment of the people's *emergence* from the Underworld. Today the dance is often performed in public with the participants dressed in the costumes of the Plains Indians.

Hopewell See *Mound Builders*.

Hopi The Hopi are the westernmost of the *pueblo* peoples. The word Hopi means 'peace', making this tribe the 'Peaceful People'. They are deeply religious and at peace with Nature, and regard themselves as the first inhabitants of America. They are also the only Indian people who have never signed a treaty of any kind with the United States Government.

The Hopi reservation is situated in the middle of the *Navajo* Reservation in the northeastern corner of Arizona. It stretches over some 631,000 acres, with 1,841,000 acres owned jointly with the Navajo. The people live, for the most part, atop three mesas, where they have withstood enemy invasions for over a thousand years. These mesas are called First, Second and Third Mesa. The major villages on First Mesa are Walpi, Hano and Sichomovi, with Pollaca located at the base. The Second Mesa villages are Shungopovi, Mishongnovi and Shipaulovi. On Third Mesa there is Old Oraibi, the longest continuously inhabited settlement in North America, together with Hotevilla and Bakavi. Meonkopi, the only village not on the mesas, is located 40 miles west of Third Mesa, near Tuba City, Arizona.

From the very beginning the Hopi resisted the whites, even killing the white Christian priests that came to try to convert them to Christianity. Today, however, white society has begun to creep onto the mesas and the young people are showing less and less interest in carrying on their ancestral tradition. The Hopi people are represented by the Tribal Council, an elected government. Their crafts include making pottery, *baskets*, silver jewelry and *kachina* dolls, and *weaving*.

It is also said that the Hopi are the best dry farmers in the world. They raise *corn*, *beans*, squash, cotton and fruit—corn is considered the 'Mother of the Hopi'—but because their land is in the high desert, the growing season is very short and rainfall is limited. This accounts for almost all of their sacred *ceremonies* being held to bring rain. Hopi life is centered around ceremonies that enable them to seek help from the supernatural forces they believe control Nature. These ceremonies are accompanied by dances and songs that take place in the plaza areas of the villages and may be viewed by the public. After a sequence of a dance has been completed, there is a brief pause when the dancers go to a prescribed rest area. Sometimes during the pauses *clowns* entertain the audience.

The fundamental basis of the Hopi religion is the *kachina* cult. Kachinas, the 'Cloud People', are supernatural beings who embody the spirits of living things as well as the spirits of Hopi ancestors who have passed on to become part of Nature. Kachinas are believed to possess special powers over Nature, especially over the weather.

The ceremonial year begins at the *winter solstice* with the *Soyal* Ceremony, which marks the return of the kachinas to the mesas from the sacred *mountains*, that is the San Francisco Peaks in Flagstaff, Arizona, some 150 miles away. It continues with the Niman or

'Home Dance' at the summer solstice, when the kachinas go to their home in the mountains once again, and ends in late November with the final and most important ceremony of all, the *Wuwuchim*. This is the time of the initiation of young men into the secret societies, ensuring the continuation of the ceremonial cycle and of the people themselves. Wuwuchim involves long, hard ceremonies that signify rebirth, and also religious instruction and tests of endurance. (See also *Bean Dance*.)

During the kachina dances, the men of the villages impersonate the Cloud People, allowing the kachinas to assume form and appear in the streets and plazas of the villages. When a Hopi impersonates a kachina, he believes that he actually becomes the kachina. Endowed with supernatural powers, he can then cure disease, bring rain, grow crops, and reinforce discipline and order within the Hopi world. It is said that there are over 500 kachinas in the Hopi spiritual hierarchy. Some kachina ceremonies are done at about the same time each year, while others are sponsored by individual families, and are called 'social dances'. These are usually given on weekends and are almost always open to the public.

Hopi cosmology is extremely complex. It tells of the Creation by *Taiowa*, the only Creator. The first world created was called Tokpela, Endless Space. There, nothing existed—no time, no space. All was in the mind of the Creator. Then Taiowa created the finite and a helper, Sotuknang, the First Power. Sotuknang, in turn, created Kokyangwuti who is called *Spider Woman*. It was she who was given dominion over the newly-created Earth and who created lifeforms out of its soil, one of which was mankind. The people of the First World could not speak and they still had a soft spot in their heads and dampness on their foreheads. They knew no sickness until evil entered into the world. It was then up to the *medicine* men to cure the illness by laying a *crystal* on one of the sacred 'centers' (chakras) of the human body for diagnosis. As a result, the people began to understand themselves and they were pure and happy.

The Second World, Tokpa, was a world where the people remained happy and multiplied. However, they soon forgot the commands of Spider Woman and began to see differences between each other. This caused the animals to go away from them and the people began to divide and separate. They started to speak different languages and became of different colors (races). There were only a few who continued to live by the rules of Creation.

This state of affairs was deemed bad by Sotuknang. So the pure people were instructed to go and live underground with the Ant People and the bad people were destroyed. When the destruction was over, the pure people emerged from under the ground and that marked the beginning of a new world, the Third World, which was called Kuskurza.

Upon this world the people spread out and multiplied and continued the process of evolution. They grew in knowledge, and created big cities, whole countries and civilizations. This led them, however, to become totally involved with their earthly plans. Once again, though, not all of the people broke the rules of the Creator. But those that did ignored not only the rules but did not perform the ceremonies and began to fight for power amongst each other.

This saddened Sotuknang and he instructed Spider Woman to get some tall plants with hollow stems and to put the pure people inside them and seal them up. Sotuknang then loosed a great flood upon the Earth and the Third World and the bad people were destroyed. This led to the Fourth World, Tuwaqachi, and the next *emergence*.

Tuwaqachi, the Fourth World, is the present world in which we are living. It is the 'World Complete'. It is not as beautiful as the other worlds and is not easy to live in. It has heat and cold, height and depth, beauty and barrenness. When it was formed, the people were told to spread out and go their separate ways and to claim the Earth for the Creator. What they chose would determine whether or not this world would survive. Each group was told to follow their own star until it stopped, marking the place for a group to settle.

The spirit Masaw was appointed by the Creator as the guardian and protector of this Fourth World. He was the first being the people met in this world and they greatly respected him. He, in turn, gave them permission to live on the land. Masaw warned that if the people became evil again then he would take over the Earth. So it is the task of the people living on the Earth to obey the rules of the Creator and live in peace and harmony. Some Hopi believe that the people on the Earth today are becoming bad again and there is great fear that the Fourth World, the last world, will be destroyed.

Horse Indians See *Tribes*.

Horses The Indians first got horses from the Spaniards. This had a tremendous effect on them, not the least of which had to do with their being able to cover greater distances in much shorter times. Also, horses were used as pack animals, enabling the Indians to facilitate moves much more easily. Some *tribes* moved frequently, as they hunted *buffalo* and other game, and had to go where the game could be found.

Furthermore, the horse made the Indian a much more effective warrior, for he could travel greater distances and get away quicker, as well as develop more powerful battle techniques—the use of the lance, for example.

In some instances, such as with the *Nez Perce* and *Chief Joseph*, horses were bred and refined, resulting in the appearance of the breed known as the Apaloosa. In this case the horse became a 'marketable' product, as well as being prize stock.

Hunkapi One of the sacred rites of the *Sioux* Indians, Hunkapi is the 'Making of Relatives' ceremony. In this rite the Sioux establish a relationship on the physical level that reflects the ever-existing relationship between man and the *Great Spirit*, whom they call *Wankan-Tankan*. The people believe that the performance of this ritual is the will of the Great Spirit.

Hunkapi was first given to the Sioux by the White Buffalo Cow Woman, though they are not the only people who claim to be the originators of the ceremony. The ceremony itself was said to have been received in a vision by a Lakota, Matohoshila (Bear Boy), who said that performing this rite would also help to make peace with the Ree nation, with whom the Sioux had long been at war.

Through the rite, three forms of peace can be established. The first is that which comes in the human soul when the existence of the Great Spirit is recognized. The second is that which comes from a loving relationship between two people. The third is that which is made between nations.

Hunkpapa See *Sioux*.

I

Iktomi, the Spider Man

Igloo Common to the *Eskimo* people of central Alaska, the igloo is a dwelling made of ice. The ice is cut into blocks which are then formed into a dome-shaped domain with an opening for a door. There is another opening in the ceiling for the release of smoke.

Iktomi Also known as The Trickster, Iktomi was a malevolent being to the Plains people. He once lived in the Sky Land, but he caused so much trouble between the *sun* and *moon* that he was banished. The Plains people say that it was Iktomi who brought all evil into the world, for wherever he went, he made trouble.

Indian Removal Act The Indian Removal Act was a decree signed into law by the United States Government in 1830. The Act made it a national policy to move Indians to lands beyond the Mississippi River. The President at the time was Andrew Jackson.

Inipi Commonly known as the 'Sweat', Inipi is a sacred ceremony of the Plains people and many other *tribes*. It is a cleansing rite that is performed prior to *ceremonies*, *vision quests*, and other social rites such as marriage.

The Sweat Lodge is a dome-shaped structure made from saplings, usually willow or aspen, shaped like a turtle to represent the North American continent, which the Indians call 'Turtle Island'. The wooden frame is covered with materials that keep in the heat and keep out the light. In the center of the lodge is a hole where rocks are placed that have been heated in a *fire* pit outside. The door of the lodge opens to the east, and a spirit path leads to an altar mound in front of the door. This mound is built from the earth removed from the lodge's center pit.

After proper prayers to the fire spirits, participants enter the Sweat Lodge. Sometimes clothing is worn, sometimes it is not. When the participants are seated inside the lodge, the rocks are placed in the pit with the proper ceremony. The lodge flap is then closed and *sage* is sprinkled on the hot rocks to rid it, and those in it, of any negative energies. Then sweetgrass is placed on the rocks to bring in good energies. Next, water is poured over the stones, and steam billows forth in the darkness.

Sweat begins to run down the faces and bodies of the participants, taking out the poisons. The *Great Spirit* is invited into the ceremony, along with the Grandfather and Grandmother Spirits and the powers of the *four directions*. During the Sweat, sacred songs are sung and prayers are said. Sometimes sage is rubbed over the bodies of the participants.

A Sweat can last for hours. Sometimes tears run down the cheeks of those in the lodge, helping to cleanse them. Should the heat become too much for a person to handle, he or she is allowed to leave the lodge and, in some cases, return later. The Sweat is not an endurance test. It is the womb of *Mother Earth*, the place where Native people go to cleanse and renew themselves and to be reborn. It is also a ceremony when healing prayers may be sent to the Great Spirit so that loved ones and all who live on the Earth might be whole. Today Indian people are allowing non-Indian people to participate in the Sweats.

Inuit See *Eskimo*.

Iroquis The Iroquis were powerful and hostile people. Before the whites came, they had pushed up from the south and overrun all of the land in what is now the Carolinas to the St. Laurence Valley. They also controlled parts of Tennessee, Virginia, and Pennsylvania as well as almost all of New York except the lower Hudson Valley. Their influence was felt as far north and west as the Huron, Erie and Ontario Lakes region.

The Iroquis made friends with the English and the Dutch and used the whites for their own purposes against their old enemies, the *Algonquin*s, against the French who were pushing south into the St.

Laurence Valley, and against the threat of the American colonists. When the American Revolution broke out, the greater part of the tribe sided with the British—only the Oneidas and the Tuscaroras of the Six Iroquis Nations supported the colonists. Four Iroquis tribes, the Mohawks, Senecas, Cayugas, and the Onondagas, fled to Canada, but later all but the Mohawks returned to fight on the side of the colonists.

After the British were defeated, the Six Iroquis Nations ceded most of the land to the United States of America. Since then they have lived in the northeastern lands only by permission of the whites, though their ancestors remain there today.

Iroquis League of Six Nations Founded by the prophet *Degandawidah*, the League was originally composed of five Indian nations: the Senecas, Cayugas, Oneidas, Mohawks and Onondagas. Later the Tuscaroras joined, making it the League of Six Nations. With the help of *Hiawatha*, Degandawidah persuaded the *tribes* to join the new Iroquis religion, a combination of Indian tradition and Christianity, as well as the League.

The tribe most resistant to joining proved to be the extremely independent Onondagas. But their doubts were erased when Degandawidah and Hiawatha entered into the territory of a murderer, Atotahro, and convinced him that he should change his ways. It was Atotahro who had previously killed Hiawatha's wife and children. He did change and became a part of the Supreme Council of the League, which he faithfully served with honor for the rest of his life.

Although the League did not fulfill all the dreams of its founders, it did become a powerful military force, going on to conquer huge areas of territory. Degandawidah called the foundation upon which he built the League 'The White Roots of Peace'.

Ishna Ta Awi Cha Lowan One of the sacred rites of the *Sioux*, Ishna Ta Awi Cha Lowan is performed to prepare a young girl for womanhood. The rite takes place after the girl's first menstrual period and marks a time of great change. She must now understand that she, like *Mother Earth*, can bear children which she must rear in a sacred manner. The girl must also learn that each month, during her menstrual period, she will come into a special power that has great influence and can take away the power of a holy man. Therefore she must be very careful.

The rites include the building of a sacred *tipi* within which the girl is purified. The pipe is smoked, and the girl is cleansed with sacred herbs, one of which is sweetgrass. She then holds a bundle of sacred things over her head and receives a blessing from the *medicine man*, who tells her to go forth in a holy manner, that is, to be humble, fruitful, and merciful to others. The young woman then eats *buffalo* meat and drinks from a bowl of water containing cherries. This bowl is also passed among the people, who each take a sip from it.

When the ceremony was finished, the girl, now a woman, comes out of the tipi to be touched by everyone. This rite brings great happiness, and ends with *feasting* and a *giveaway*.

Isleta Isleta is the southernmost *pueblo* in New Mexico, located some 12 miles south of Albuquerque. There are about 2,000 Isleta people living there on a reservation of some 211,000 acres. Isletas are farmers who raise cattle and grow large grape vineyards. It is thought that they learned how to grow grapes from the Franciscan monks who came from California and established a monastery at Isleta around 1629.

The pueblo was destroyed by the Spaniards in 1681 as punishment for having participated in the Great Pueblo Revolt, but the village was rebuilt and resettled in the eighth century by the *Tewas*, who had begun to live with the *Hopi*. The Isletas speak Tewa and belong to the Kiowa-Tanoan linguistic family.

J

Chief Joseph of the Nez Perce

Captain Jack Captain Jack was a *Modoc* who led his men into the lava beds of northern California. He was also a great leader in the Modoc War. It is said that he took such a strong stand that it took 1,500 soldiers to drive him out. He was hanged at Ft Klamath on 3 October 1873.

James, Marlise See *Wabun Wind*.

Jamestown Colony See *Powhatan*.

Jicarillo See *Apache*.

Jimson Weed See *Datura*.

Chief Joseph Joseph was chief of the *Nez Perce* Indians of Washington state at the time of their conflict with the whites. He was called 'In-mut-too-yah-lat-lat' by his tribe, meaning 'Thunder-Traveling-over-the-Mountain'. He was a devout Christian and most beloved leader.

The Nez Perce, divided into Upper and Lower Bands, had always been at peace with the white man. These were the Indians who had treated the Lewis and Clark expedition with such great kindness and hospitality. After meeting with them in 1873 the Indian commission was so impressed that the commissioners petitioned President Grant to issue an executive order setting aside the Wallowa Valley for them. But in 1875, at the insistence of Governor Grover, the President rescinded this order.

The Upper Band had accepted and signed the treaties offered for their land by the United States government, but Joseph and the Lower Nez Perce had accepted no treaty goods. The government then claimed the Upper Band had made a treaty for the Lower Band's land as well, and that the Indians had sold the Wallowa Valley. The Indians had been greatly mistreated by the whites who had settled on their land—they had been murdered, and their stock and *horses* stolen. Two Indians had even been tied up and beaten by white ranchers. It seemed as if there was no recourse or justice left to them. Yet Joseph preached peace and restraint to his people. General Howard gave them only 30 days to gather their stock and horses for removal to Lapwai Reservation. Yet, to avoid bloodshed, Joseph prepared to move. He knew that he could not hope to defeat the United States and that fighting would only result in the slaughter of his people.

A statement he made at this time shows what kind of man he was: 'I said in my heart that, rather than have war, I would give up my country. I would give up everything rather than have the blood of the white men upon the hands of my people.'

Things began to change drastically, however, when the people of Chief White Bird, a leader of the Upper Band, were gathered together in camp with Joseph's people. While Joseph was away from camp, the young men began gambling and talking wild. Three warriors rode out and killed the rancher who had beaten the Indians. Now all restraint was gone. They killed three more whites and returned to camp to boast of their experience. Soon other Nez Perce joined them and they went out and killed other people who had wronged and cheated them.

When Joseph returned to camp, it had been done, and there was no going back. Knowing that soldiers would surely come and punish them, he schooled his men for battle. Less than half had guns, but the Nez Perce were to prove to be outstanding marksmen. Chief Joseph began to show his generalship. If he must fight, then he would pick the battlefield. He moved his people to White Bird Canyon, and there waited for the troops.

Although he had never fired a gun in anger against a white man, he was not to be taken by surprise. He carefully hid some of his men for an ambush and placed others on horseback in a side canyon. In spite of the Indian scouts working for the army, 90 infantrymen came straight into the trap and were surrounded on three sides. They tried to retreat but for the Indians it was like a shooting gallery. Not one of the troops came out alive. Joseph knew that he could no longer stay in that area. It was then that he began his famous 1,200 mile trek with the tribe's women and children and all their livestock, doubling back and forth and passing through high mountain passes on what was thought of as an impossible journey. In the next 100 days, the Nez Perce band fought 17 battles and conducted themselves outstandingly. They did no scalping and when they took women prisoners, they treated them with respect. They bought and paid for supplies at trading posts, often at exceedingly high prices, and on occasion, gave water to a wounded enemy.

After reaching the Bear Paw Mountains in Montana, Joseph felt that they were safe. They camped less than 35 miles from the Canadian border—a chance for their wounded to recover and to rest their weary people and livestock. However, they were attacked by troops commanded by General Miles. Although they fought them off, Miles demanded unconditional surrender. Joseph refused, saying that he was willing to return to his homeland and live in peace.

This refusal resulted in Miles ordering a cannon to be used against the Indians. The Nez Perce would not agree to any surrender, and the fighting went on. Joseph's band could have escaped into Canada, but they would not leave their wounded or the women and children— they had never heard of an Indian recovering in the hands of a white man. Finally, on 5 October, General Howard arrived and immediately sent a Nez Perce scout from the Lapwai Reservation to offer Joseph new terms to surrender. The next day, after almost four months of fighting, Joseph's small brave band gave up.

After the surrender, Joseph had only 79 warriors, 46 of whom were wounded. I should like to be able to say that the Nez Perce were returned to their reservation according to what was promised them. But it was not to be. Instead, they were moved to the Tongue River in Montana, then to Bismarck, North Dakota, and finally to Leavenworth, Kansas, where many of them sickened and died. General Miles was opposed to the government breaking his word in this way, but that changed nothing. The Nez Perce were moved to Indian Territory, that is Oklahoma, where they were offered some sagebrush and sand as a permanent reservation.

Joseph made many trips to Washington, asking to be returned to his homeland, but all his words fell on deaf ears. In 1879 he made a statement that was published in *The North American Review*:

Let me be a free man, free to travel, free to stop, free to work, free to trade where I choose, free to choose my own teachers, free to follow the religion of my fathers, free to talk, think and act for myself, and I will obey every law or submit to the penalty.

In 1881, the government decided to return the survivors of the Looking Glass and White Bird Bands to Idaho, while Joseph and his people were sent to the Colville Reservation in Washington state.

Chief Joseph died there in 1904 and was buried at Nespelem, Washington. It is said that his war strategies are still taught at West Point Military Academy. The most famous words attributed to him are: 'I will fight no more forever.'

K

Kokopelli, the Hump-backed Flute Player

Kachina *Hopi* kachinas are 'supernatural beings' who are at the very center of Hopi religious life. They embody the spirits of living things and also the spirits of Hopi ancestors.

Kachinas are believed to possess special powers over Nature, especially the weather, which is of particular concern to these people who live in the harsh desert environment of northeastern Arizona. They guard and protect the Hopi, and ensure the fertility of the crops. The kachina cult involves kachina *dances* that play a prominent role in Hopi ceremonial life. During these dances, Hopi men—and sometimes women—impersonate the kachinas, believing they actually become the kachina involved.

Because of the complex needs of Hopi life, there are over 500 different kinds of kachina. Each has special markings, colors and decorations. Kachina dances are held from the time of the *winter solstice* in December through the summer solstice in June.

The carving of kachina dolls from the root of a cottonwood tree is a method of teaching Hopi children about the kachina spirits. The dolls, which range from the most primitive to the most elaborately beautiful, range from an inch to a foot in length. The finished dolls are decorated with a variety of identifying materials that include furs, *feathers*, bird beaks, animal claws and talons, and head-dresses.

The Hopi believe that each kachina represents a different spirit and that the kachinas taught them to farm, dance, hunt, weave, and make their silver overlay jewelry. Kachinas are also credited with bringing good times, prosperity and joyful peace to the Hopi people. Their most important gift, however, is the life-giving rain.

When the people became evil and strayed off the good path, the kachinas left the mesas and refused to return. So it was in the people's best interest to work out a compromise, which came when the kachina spirits allowed the Indians to impersonate them. Now the kachinas are said to return to the mesas during the *Soyal* ceremony in December. Afterwards, they go once again to their home in the sacred *mountains* at the end of the Niman or 'Home Dance' in June. (See also *Hopi*.)

The following is an explanation of some of the most important kachinas.

Ahola Ahola is an important chief kachina and is the 'Ancient One' of the Kachina Clan. He performs a rite that involves the magical slowing of the passage of the *sun*, and is also the chief of the Powamu ceremony, also known as the *Bean Dance*.

As the Ancient One, Ahola led the people from the San Francisco Peaks both eastward to the Mississippi River and westward to where their houses still stand.

Angak'china The so-called Long-haired Kachina is another that is found throughout the Southwestern *pueblos*. There are many varieties of long-haired kachinas. They appear in groups and sing a wonderfully melodious song. Their dances always bring rain.

Angwusi Angwusi is known as the *Crow* Kachina. He is also one of those who make war on the *clowns*.

Chaveyo This kachina can appear at any time during the spring. He is a giant and is very popular with the people because of his cantankerousness. When a Hopi fails to meet his obligations in the community or breaks any rules of conduct, Chaveyo comes to show him the errors of his ways.

Corn Kachina The Corn Dancer appears in a spring dance and dances to promote the growth of *corn*.

Crow Mother Crow Mother is called Angwushahai-i by the Hopi. On Third Mesa she imitates and disciplines the children. Crow Mother appears in all white at the end of the Powamu ceremony, and also appears, at times, as the Crow Bride, bearing a large tray of *corn* sprouts. Women then take the corn sprouts from her tray.

Deer Kachina The Deer Kachina is very popular with the Hopi. It is said that he has power over the rain. When he dances it is also for the purpose of increasing the supply of this animal for *food*.

Eototo The Eototo Kachina appears every year on each of the three mesas. He is considered to be the spiritual 'counterpart' of the village chief and in this capacity he is called the 'father' of the kachinas. He is the chief of all kachinas, is thoroughly familiar with every ceremony and appears in all of the major ones.

Hemis Hemis is one of the most beautiful and best known of all the Hopi kachinas. He is most often seen during the Niman Ceremony when the kachinas come into the plaza for the first time, carrying corn plants from the first harvest of the year. The plants, in turn, are given to the people in the audience, and will sometimes have kachina dolls or other gifts tied to them.

Hon Kachina Commonly known as the Bear Kachina, it is said that Hon has such tremendous strength that he can cure the sick. He has *bear* footprints painted on either cheek.

Hopi Shalako Taka Otherwise known as the Hopi Cloud Man, the Shalako represents all of the Cloud People. The *Zunis* also have a *Shalako* that appears every year, although the Hopi Shalako appears very rarely.

Kau-a-Kachin Mana Kau-a-Kachin Mana is one of the most unique versions of the Kachina Mother. She carries a basket during the plaza dances and occasionally kneels and makes a sound with a notched stick called a 'rasper' which is placed on the basket and scraped with an animal scapula.

Kokopelli This kachina is known as the Hump-backed Flute Player. He is phallic in nature and is found throughout the pueblos of the Southwest. He usually appears in the mixed kachina dances and sometimes in a night dance. He is considered a seducer of young girls, the bringer of babies, a teacher of hunting and of carving kachina dolls.

Koyemsi Commonly called the Mudheads, Koyemsi are the best-known of all kachinas. They appear in all the ceremonies as clowns, announcers of the dances and drummers, as well as in other roles. They play games with the audience and the winners are rewarded with gifts of food or clothing. Mudheads also appear in the night dances.

Kweo Kweo is the Wolf Kachina. He is a hunter and a side dancer at the Soyohim Ceremony, often along with the Deer and Antelope

Kachinas. He is offered prayer feathers and cornmeal by the people so that he will help them to secure enough game for food.

Masau'u Sometimes known as the Skeleton Kachina, Masau'u is the only kachina who does not go home to the San Francisco Peaks during the Home Dance, and may dance at any time during the year. He is also the Death Kachina and often does many things in reverse, for example coming down a ladder backwards or walking backwards, for the World of the Dead is contrary to the physical world. He comes with a female kachina known as the Masau'u Mana. She is a bringer of rain.

Mongwa Mongwa is the Great Horned Owl Kachina. He is best known for his continuing war with the clowns for their mischievous behavior. Mongwa is a discipline kachina.

Nuvak'chin Mana Commonly known as the Snow Maiden, Nuvak'chin Mana is one of the Kachina Manas. She makes prayers for the coming of cold weather in hopes that snow will come and bring moisture to the earth for the coming year. The Snow Maiden comes during the Niman or Home Dance.

Patung Patung is also known as the Squash Kachina and is primarily a runner.

Snake Dancers The Snake Dancers, also known as Chusona, are the most intriguing of all kachinas. They carry snakes in their mouths and hands during the Snake Dance, which is largely a secret dance held once in the summertime for bringing rain. The public part of the dance is currently closed to viewing by non-Indian people.

Sohu Sohu is the Star Kachina. He often appears in the mixed kachina dances but never alone.

Tawa Tawa is the Sun Kachina, representing the spirit of the sun.

Tocha Commonly called the Hummingbird Kachina, Tocha is a favorite kachina. He enters the *kiva*, gives out a shrill call and dances with great speed.

Wiharu Commonly known as the White Ogre, this kachina comes to frighten the children into being well-behaved. He carries various items in his hands, such as a *bow and arrow*, designed to get the children's attention.

Wuyak-kuita Wuyak-kuita appears in every ceremony as a guardian.

Karok The Karok were a tribe of salmon fishermen who lived along the Klamath River between the Yuroks and Hupas to the south and the Shastas to the north. They bought *canoes* from the Yuroks and their culture was similar to that of their Yurok and Hupa neighbors. They called themselves 'Arra-Arra', which meant 'humans'.

Kikmongwi Kikmongwi are village chiefs. Each chief is called 'the Father of the People' by the *Hopi*.

Kinnikinic Kinnikinic is a smoking mixture used by Native people in the sacred pipe ceremony (see *Pipes*). It includes *sage*, white clover, *bear* berry leaves and *mullein* leaves.

Kiowa The Kiowa are a tribe of Native American people who lived on the southern Great Plains of the North American continent. Since 1868 they have shared a reservation with the *Comanche* Indians between the Washita and Red rivers in southwest Oklahoma. They are divided into seven bands, one of which is the Kiowa *Apaches*, a small southern Athabascan band who speak an Apachean *language*.

In earlier times, the Kiowa were typical of nomadic Plains *tribes*. Once they acquired *horses* from the Spaniards, they became *buffalo* hunters on horseback. They had no agriculture, and their dwellings, for the most part, were skin *tipis*. They had warrior societies whose members attained their status from battle exploits.

The Kiowa spirituality placed tremendous value on dreams and visions which they believed—and still believe—gave them supernatural powers to be used in various aspects of life, including war, hunting and *healing*. The tribe possessed ten *medicine* bundles which they believed protected them. The Kiowa also did the *Sun Dance* and were instrumental, along with the Comanche, in spreading the peyote religion.

Another Kiowa ceremonial involved pictographic artwork that was done twice each year. Its purpose was to log important tribal events. These 'calendric' histories were painted on animal skins by an artist of the tribe.

Today the Kiowa number approximately 3,000.

Kiva The kiva is a subterranean ceremonial chamber of the *pueblo* Indians, the site of secret sacred rituals. The oldest kivas were circular but now they are rectangular and built on a straight north/south line. Kivas are hidden among the dwellings of the plaza. Most are at least half or totally underground, having been dug into the rocks or stony red clay of the valleys. Their flat roofs are supported by log beams covered with adobe.

The kiva is entered by descending ladders that can be more than 30 feet long and are placed in openings left by trap doors. In the middle of the kiva area is a shallow *fire* pit. As there is no chimney, the smoke goes out of the trap door.

The actual number of kivas in a plaza may vary, depending upon the size of the pueblo and the number of ceremonial groups. The village of Old Oraibi on Third Mesa, for example, has 13 kivas, and there are 33 kivas in total on the three *Hopi* mesas. Some are small but others are very large. Kiva walls are decorated with painted symbols and an altar. An interesting feature of the kiva is the 'Sipapus', representing the original *Sipapu*, which is a low platform located behind the ladder. Above the platform is a small round hole, representing the beginning and the end and man's point of origin and departure. The kiva altar may be simple or elaborate and is the place for bowls, prayer sticks, *rattles*, *pipes*, *feathers* and animal skins.

For the most part, it is the men who perform the secret rituals in the kiva, but women do bring in *food* and, at times, are allowed to see parts of the sacred *ceremonies*. On occasion, the women enter the kiva to conduct the rituals pertaining to the various women's societies.

Kokopelli See *Kachina*.

Kokyangwuti See *Spider Woman*.

L

Lance

Lalakonti See *Basket Dance.*

Lame Deer John Fire Lame Deer was a full-blooded Lakota *Sioux* born on the Rosebud Reservation in South Dakota. He was a *medicine man*, a healer, a seeker of visions, and *shaman*. During his life he held many jobs including potato picker, sign painter, tribal policeman, bootlegger and 'sheepherder', to use the Native American term. But his life was eventually dedicated to his *medicine*, which he received in a vision during his childhood. Lame Deer did a great deal to share his tradition with all people.

Lance See *Ceremonial Lance.*

Language There were some 300 languages spoken among the Indians when Columbus arrived in the New World, but only about 50 to 100 survive today. Some of them are so complex that they can hardly be translated into English—the *Hopi* language is an example—and most Indians cannot understand the language of other *tribes*, for the differences between them are so pronounced.

Several classifications have been made of Indian languages, the main linguistic groups being Algonquian, Athapascan, Siouan,

Tanoan, Muskhogean, Caddoan and Shoshonean. The Algonquian tribes once inhabited most of what is now the United States. Among them were the *Chippewas, Cheyennes*, and the Delawares. The Athapascan tribes were found scattered from central Alaska and northwestern Canada to Mexico in the south, and from the Hudson Bay to the Pacific Ocean. The Athapascans are sub-divided into groups in New Mexico, Arizona and Utah, and parts of Colorado, Texas and Mexico. The Siouan tribes were found from the Mississippi River to the Rockies. There were also groups in Virginia, North and South Carolina, southern Mississippi, eastern Montana and Arkansas. (Today the *Sioux* tribes are found in the Dakotas and in some of the other states of the Great Plains, further west than the Mississippi.) The Tanoan tribes are the ancestral stock of the *pueblos* of New Mexico. They speak three tongues: Tewa, Tiwa and Towa. The Muskhogean tribes live on the Gulf Coast, in southern Appalachia, at the mouth of the Mississippi River, Florida, and Georgia, Tennessee and Kentucky. Caddoan was the language of the people of the Southern Plains and those living further north towards the Missouri River. Shoshonean was the language of the Great Basin and Lower Plateau areas of Nevada, Colorado and Utah. Some Shoshonean-speaking tribes also lived in southern California and spread eastward into Texas.

The wide range of Indian languages indicates that the Native people once roamed over large areas, although by the time the whites arrived they had firmly established their homes in the lands they laid claim to.

Little Dog Little Dog was a Brule *Sioux* who was born in 1848. He fought in a war party the first time at the age of 16. The next year, he led a war party against infantry troops, during which he counted three coups (see *Coup Sticks*) and was wounded three times. Because of the death of his sister, he fought alone against the *Pawnee*. Little Dog scouted for General Crook and participated in 45 battles and 15 horse raids.

Llaneros See *Apache*.

Logan Logan was a chief of the Mingoes, who lived in what is now the state of Ohio. He had always counseled his people to keep peace with the white man, and was a man of extreme honesty. During the French and Indian Wars and the *Pontiac* uprising, Logan held his people at peace, and was spoken of as a friend of the white man. Although there were some incidents that the settlers blamed on the Indians, there were plenty of lawless whites who could have been responsible. So, in the spring of 1774, it was with nothing more to go on than his hatred of the Indians that Captain Cresap gathered together a large band of eager killers and pounced on the first Indians he came across.

These were Logan's family, who were camped at Yellow Creek. They were all murdered. Ironically, the chief had been away at a peace council where he had persuaded the tribe to agree to peace with the white man. On his return, he found his reward for being kind to the whites. Taking a party of eight or ten warriors, he set out to kill the settlers and drive them out of the border settlements. In reply, an army of some 3,000 men was raised by Lord Dunmore, Governor of Virginia. To surround Logan, he sent 1,500 men by a northern route under General Andrew Lewis and led the other army himself. It was at Point Pleasant, Ohio, that General Lewis's army engaged Logan's band as well as the war party of Cronstalk, chief of the Shawnees.

For a while it looked as if the Virginians would be defeated. But then the Indians were pushed back to some fallen timbers that they had arranged for fortifications. They held out until General Lewis sent some men behind them. Thinking that these were reinforcements from Lord Dunmore, the Indians retreated. At this, Dunmore sent a messenger telling General Lewis to cease from further battles. Lewis, however, insisted on pursuing the Indians and the Governor had to go so far as to threaten to kill him before he finally stopped. The Governor then sent a message to the Indians, offering them peace.

Cornstalk and the other chiefs agreed to come into the peace conference, but Logan refused. Governor Dunmore sent a messenger to Logan to find out his intentions, since Logan was a powerful chief and could easily lead men on the warpath again, and Logan replied that he had been a friend to the white man, but had been betrayed.

Peace, however, was desirable. Logan's words softened the hearts of Thomas Jefferson and others. Impressed by his sincerity, they compared his speech to those of the great Greek orators. This was the start of the peace process, and treaties were ultimately signed. Logan lived on and acted as a peace representative for his people at future times. But, sadly, his grief stayed with him until his death.

M

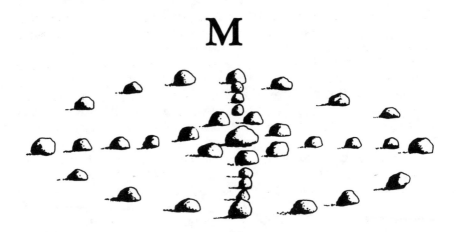

Medicine Wheel

Mad Bear Andersen Mad Bear Andersen was an *Iroquis medicine man*, noted healer, and an interpreter/teacher of the prophecies of his people.

Maestros See *Yaqui*.

Mahad'yuni Mahad'yuni, meaning 'Hands-Show-the-Way', also known as Evelyn Eaton, was a pipe woman, healer, author and teacher. She was born in 1902 in Switzerland to Canadian parents and educated in England, Canada and France, where she lived as a struggling young writer until 1936, although her first poem had been published when she was only eight years old. She became an American citizen in 1944 and served as a war correspondent, then later taught at Columbia University, Mary Washington University, Sweet Briar College, Ohio State, Pershing College and Deep Springs College.

  In 1960, Mahad'yuni moved to Owens Valley, California, where she began to study the ways of the Native Americans with Paiute and Arapaho *medicine* people. She had both *Micmac* and Malisite blood, although she did not learn of her Indian heritage until she was an adult. She worked with the Sweat Lodge (see *Inipi*) and other *ceremonies,* and was a tribal *grandmother* to the *Bear Tribe Medicine Society* in Spokane, Washington, and the author of several books, including *Snowy Earth Comes Gliding, The Shaman and the Medicine Wheel* and *I Send a Voice.* Mahad'yuni died in 1983.

Mandan See *Medicine Pole.*

Mangus Colorado This outstanding leader of the *Apache* people was a powerfully built man, six feet five inches tall. Besides his great strength, he also possessed great intelligence. He became a hard-hitting war chief, fighting across Arizona, Texas, New Mexico and down into Mexico.

Mangus Colorado belonged to the band of Mimbreno Apaches who once lived peacefully with their Mexican neighbors at the village of Santa Rita. The Mexicans were miners, and the Apaches allowed them to live in their territory. But the government of Chihuahua had passed a law paying bounty on Apache scalps, and a group of 17 American trappers under James Johnson decided that here was some quick money. So they made a deal with the Mexicans at Santa Rita and then invited the Apaches to a fiesta. After the Apaches had eaten and gotten drunk on *mescal* (peyote), the Mexicans brought out bags of *corn* that they said were gifts. When the Apaches gathered around the corn, the Americans fired cannons in their midst. These cannons were loaded with nails and all sorts of scrap iron, broken up for that purpose. After this, Johnson and his men, along with the Mexicans, finished off many more unarmed Indians.

Mangus Colorado had not trusted the Mexicans who had invited the Apaches to this so-called fiesta, and he would drink no mescal. But Juan José, the chief of the Apache band, had got drunk and was in no condition to help his people. Four hundred Apaches died that day. Among the dead were Mangus Colorado's two wives. Knowing that there was nothing much that he could do at the time, he simply grabbed a small Apache child and ran to escape the slaughter, his heart black with revenge.

Finally the time for revenge did come, when a group of Mexicans set out from Santa Rita in search of late supply wagons. Mangus Colorado let them get three days out. Then he chose a valley he knew they had to pass through, concealed his warriors behind trees and boulders on both sides and at each end, and attacked them when they stopped to rest. The 400 Mexicans were armed but had no chance of fighting their way out. They tried to escape, running in every direction, but the Apaches picked them off. Mangus let the padre and a few others escape, however, so they could tell other Mexicans to stay out of Apache territory, and that this was repayment for the treachery of Santa Rita.

Mangus Colorado then continued the raids against the Mexicans, going deep into Mexico. In 1846, when the United States declared war on Mexico, he and his people offered to help. They sold *horses* and mules to the army, and even offered to send their warriors along. At this time, Americans could travel safely through Apache land as long as they were just passing through.

At first Colorado's bands had fought against the white settlers, but there were always more coming, and the chief knew that his people could not fight forever. He wanted a fair peace for them, and so when the army contacted him to make a peace parley, he was ready to respond. Cochise and other chiefs warned him that the white man might not be sincere, and that this could be a trick to capture him. But Mangus Colorado wanted peace, so he went to the camp of Captain Shirland under a white flag of truce. Despite this symbol, when he arrived in the camp he was immediately taken prisoner. When the commanding officer, Colonel West, heard of his capture, he rushed to the camp. He ordered two soldiers to guard Mangus Colorado, then to make it look as if he were trying to escape and kill him. In the night, one guard heated his bayonet until it was red hot and placed it against the leg of the sleeping chief. When Mangus leaped up, both guards fired, killing him. Thus ended the life of a great Indian leader.

Mangus Colorado was able to organize and coordinate Indians from all over the area of which he was chief. He loved his people and worked hard for them. He was intelligent, too, and would be a fine man for any people to remember. The Indians cherish his memory.

Manitonquat Manitonquat, also known as Medicine Story, is a Keeper of the Lore of the Wampanoag people, director of 'Another Place' in New Hampshire, and founder of the Mettanokit community. He is also the author of *Return To Creation*. Medicine Story travels extensively, sharing his tradition with people of all races.

Masaw See *Hopi*, *Tablets*.

Masks Masks are worn by members of secret *medicine* societies, dancers, and some *kachinas*. Usually carved from wood by the *Iroquois* and the *pueblo* people of the Southwest, especially the *Hopi*, they are worn while curing the sick, to alleviate pain and suffering, and for exorcisms. The best-known mask wearers are those of the False Face Societies of the Iroquois. These societies are secret, but membership can be gained by dreaming of a particular mask or taking part in the society's *ceremonies*.

Massasoit Massasoit was the first Indian, or 'sachem', known to the

Plymouth Colony and was of the Wampanoag tribe. He was introduced to the colonists by Samoset and Sqanto, the latter previously a slave who had been captured by an early sailing vessel that had visited that shore. Massasoit came to the colony with 60 men. Sqanto explained that they were friendly and wished peace. An agreement of peace was made, and Massasoit gave the Plymouth Colony a large tract of land. This was land whose former inhabitants had died of pestilence. The Indians established trade with the colony, trading furs and seed *corn*. Massasoit lived with the colonists for 50 years, and maintained peace. The surrounding chiefs who gave him allegiance spoke always of his kindness to them, and while he was a great chief, having many settlements under him, he never possessed any great wealth himself—the only adornment that distinguished him from others was a bone bead necklace.

Mata Tipila Mata Tipila, which means 'Bear Lodge', is the name given to Devil's Tower, a unique stone tower in Wyoming. Named Devil's Tower in 1875, it is 1,267 feet high and is located in the northeastern corner of the state. It is sacred to the *Sioux* Indians.

The Sioux tell of a warrior who would go out into the wilderness so that he might be in solitude. On one occasion, the warrior took his *buffalo* skull and went to the base of Mata Tipila. After two days of praying, he suddenly found himself on top of the steep rock tower. He was afraid because he did not know how to get down. But after falling into a deep sleep, he awakened to find himself once again at the base of the tower, standing at the door of a *bear's* lodge. He then knew that the cracks in the rock were made from the bear's claws.

Since that time, the Sioux have called the rock tower Mata Tipila. The buffalo skull taken to the top of the rock by the warrior may still be seen there.

Matachin Society The Matachin Society is a male *dance* group of the *Yaqui* Indians of Arizona. Through the strong Catholic influence on the tribe's ceremonials, the members of the society are referred to as 'soldiers of the Virgin' (Mary). They dance during the Easter *ceremonies*, led by the 'maestros' or Yaqui priests, and in opposition to another male society called the Fariseos. The Fariseos impersonate the persecutors of Jesus and their patron saint is Judas. The Matachin dancers wear head-dresses covered with paper flowers and ribbons and carry wands decorated with colored *feathers*. The younger boys wear white dresses and act as guardians of the Virgin Mary. On Holy Saturday, the Matachins defend the church against attack by the Fariseos and symbolically kill them with flowers which represent divine blessings. The *masks* and weapons are later burned on a pyre with a Judas figure.

Medicine Medicine is all that is sacred, mysterious, supernatural or spiritual to the Indian people. To them, medicine was practiced in many ways, including performing *healing*, having the knowledge of good and bad omens, and protection from evil spirits and psychic attack, gaining power from animals, plants, stars and *ceremonies*, and gaining personal energy. A person's psychic skills were his or her 'medicine'. All *tribes* had *medicine men* and/or *women*. A medicine person is the same as a *shaman*.

Medicine Bag The medicine bag, common to most Indian peoples, is used for carrying sacred objects, *corn* pollen, special stones, animal claws, bird talons, sacred herbs, or any object that is prized by an individual. The bag is carried on the person or worn around the neck at all times. It serves a variety of purposes that include being in close contact with one's totem or one's *medicine*, and being protected from harm.

The medicine bag may also become part of what is known as the medicine bundle. The bundle can be wrapped in hide or cloth, and may contain, besides the medicine bag, *pipes*, *fetishes*, minerals, or any other objects that are considered necessary for making good medicine.

The medicine bag is rarely opened in front of others unless it is for ceremonial purposes.

Medicine Bundle See *Medicine Bag*.

Medicine Eagle, Brooke Brooke Medicine Eagle is the great-great grand niece of *Chief Joseph*, the *Nez Perce* leader and holy man. She is trained both in the traditions of her people, and in Western psychology and bodywork. Brooke lectures throughout the world.

Medicine Man/Woman Medicine people are holy men/women of mystery who served as prophets, soothsayers, moral leaders and healers of the tribe. Because of their service as healers, the French called them 'médecins' or 'doctors', and the word *medicine* became applicable to everything pertaining to these holy men/women, as well as to anything that the Indians held sacred.

Medicine Pole Medicine poles were used by the Mandans, who were a Plains people living near the upper Missouri River area. The Mandans used the medicine pole in the same manner as the *totem pole* of the northwestern *tribes*, that is, as a symbol of the totem animals, which were a source of power and prestige for a family. The pole was taken in at night and during bad weather. It was decorated with various animals and colors, depending on the tastes of the family involved.

Medicine Story See *Manitonquat*.

Medicine Wheel The ancient medicine wheels were stone *circles* left by the nomadic peoples of the Great Plains and western Canada. Large effigy figures were traced out in a field with stone alignments and a number of enigmatic large wheel patterns. It is only in modern times that these have come to be known as medicine wheels—we do not know what the ancient people called them.

The best-known example of such an ancient site is the Bighorn Medicine Wheel in north central Wyoming, between Sheridan and Lovell, just south of the Montana border. The most elaborate and best preserved wheel, the Bighorn wheel consists of a hollowed-out central cairn that is about four meters in diameter. From this radiates 28 spokes, with each of them terminating in a crude circle. Around the periphery of this rim are six smaller cairns, one of which, in the southwest, lies at the end of an extended spoke outside the main circle. The Bighorn Medicine Wheel is special to the Plains *tribes* and is claimed by the Arapahoe, *Shoshone*, *Cheyenne*, *Crow* and *Sioux* for certain, and probably by others as well.

The exact use and purpose of the medicine wheels is not known, but it is supposed that they served calendric and ceremonial purposes. Some wheels, such as that of the Bighorn, marked the summer solstice and certain stars of midsummer dawn. The brightest stars in the sky at the latitude of the Big Horn Mountains are Aldeberan in Taurus, Rigel in Orion, and Sirius, and these are also the only ones that rose near dawn in the few months of the year when the high-altitude site could have been occupied.

Today the medicine wheel is used by some tribes as a ceremonial tool. One example of this is in the work of *Sun Bear*. This is his view regarding the medicine wheel, the sacred Circle of Life:

> Life goes on in a circle, a medicine wheel. We humans are one part of the circle, but not the only part. The minerals, the plants, the people of the water, the winged ones, the four-leggeds, the spirit keepers, the powers of the directions, the times and the seasons are also part of this great circle. We are their relatives, and they are ours. Together we have been placed on our common Mother Earth to learn harmony with the Great Spirit, the Creator.

Mesa See *Hopi*.

Mescal Mescal, *Sophora secundiflora*, is intimately connected with peyote, being the hallucinogen that is present in the peyote cactus button. The Indians often refer to it as 'the plant that gives sleep' or 'the plant that shows the way'. It is found in the barren, rocky terrains of Texas and New Mexico. In the spring, mescal bushes are hung with clusters of pale lavender blossoms that ripen into long pods in the autumn. The *beans* inside are pierced with a hot awl and are then strung into necklaces. The piercing of the pods must be done outside on a windy day so that the poisonous fumes will not affect the worker. Women do not do this work and most *tribes* do not allow women to wear the mescal necklaces. Sometimes the ripe black beans are strung along with *beads* and sometimes alone. The strands are worn over the right shoulder and under the left arm. The wearing of mescal beans is an expression of one's 'Indianness'. The potency of mescal may differ from season to season and depends upon the quality of the soil and the climate. The usual sacrament consists of the ingestion of four 'buttons', the safe limit that may be taken without serious side-effects.

Mescaleros See *Apache*.

Metacom See *King Philip*.

Meteor's Child See *Pahotakawa*.

Meteorites Meteorites were sacred to the Skidi band of the *Pawnee* Indians. They called them 'feather head-dress stars'. The Skidi believed that at the end of the world, the stars would come to the Earth and mix among the people, giving the message that the people must get ready to be turned into stars.

It is also thought that the war bonnets of the Plains people represented a comet or meteorite. A meteor was a visiting star that brought messages from friends in the direction from which it came. Sweat Lodge stones (see *Inipi*) were said to have the same power as that inherent in meteorites. When placed on a hill, meteorites would return to the sky.

Metis The term 'Metis' is used today to indicate people of mixed blood. However, the original Metis were Indians who were part French. They were called 'half-burned wood men' by the *Chippewas*, due to their part light, part dark skin. Some Metis have adopted Indian customs and speak a *language* that is a mixture of French and English. Their legends are filled with European influences, but the Metis are very proud of their Indian heritage.

Micanopy See *Osceola*.

Micmac The Micmac, whose name means 'Allies', are a tribe of *Algonquin* stock who live in Nova Scotia, Prince Edward Island, Cape Breton Island and New Brunswick. They were the tribe that Cabot found in 1497 and the three Indians he took back to England with him were probably Micmacs. The Micmacs were expert fishermen and canoeists, and fierce warriors who sided with the French in the French and Indian wars.

Midway Star See *South Star.*

Milky Way Native Americans have a strong relationship with the heavens, particularly the bright mist stretching across the night sky that we call the Milky Way. To the Skidi *Pawnee* Indians of Nebraska, the stars of the Milky Way were a long white road across the heavens where the wind passes, the path taken by spirits as they leave the Earth. A Pawnee legend says that the Milky Way was formed by the dust that was left from a race between a *buffalo* and a horse.

The Milky Way was also considered the path into the spirit world by the *Navajo*, who called it 'the Rainbow Bridge', the bridge between the Earth and the sky.

Mingo See *Logan.*

Miniconjou See *Sioux.*

Mississippians See *Mound Builders.*

Moccasins Moccasins were hand-made foot coverings worn by all Indian people. The footlets were made from smoke-tanned or regular deerskin (see *Buckskin*) and were often beaded with various designs for decoration.

Modoc The Modocs, whose name means 'Southerners', are of Penutian stock and their *language* is similar to that of the Klamath tribe of Oregon. They resisted being put on reservations, and fought fiercely, led by their chief, *Captain Jack*. In the Modoc War of 1872–3, they holed up in the region of basalt rocks called the Lava Beds, hiding in the rocks and caves. After their surrender, many of the leaders were hanged. Part of the tribe was moved to Indian Territory in Oklahoma; the others were settled on the Klamath Reservation where their descendants live today.

Mogollon The Mogollons were an ancient culture of Native Americans who lived in the region from northern Mexico up through north central New Mexico, and eventually blended with the *Anasazi*. They were excellent dry farmers who constructed irrigation canals to help ensure good harvests, and were also excellent potters and artisans.

Mohave The Mohave tribe is part of the *tribes* that live on both sides of the Colorado River. The Mohaves are known for their handsome physical appearance and their bravery. Their *food* consists of pinon nuts, fish, melons, pumpkins, squash, *beans*, and *corn*. In the old days, they would paint and tattoo their bodies for *ceremonies*. They lived in mud and stick houses, cremated their dead and stored their grain in round, flat-roofed structures. The tribe resisted the invasion of the Spanish and the white man's way of life, though it was finally forced on them. Today the Mohaves share a reservation with the Chemehuevis in Arizona.

Mohawk See *Iroquis*.

Montezuma Montezuma is a Southwestern cultural hero, not to be confused with the Aztec emperor of the same name. The *Papago* Indians of Arizona call Monezuma 'First Man', creator of humans and animals and maker of the 'Great Eagle'. Even though he died four times, he returned to life. He taught the people how to live, then departed for his house in the Underworld in the south, never to return to Earth again.

Moon The moon, called Grandmother Moon by most, plays an important role in the lives of Indian peoples. Most Indians considered the moon to be the patron of women and all crops, particularly *corn*. It ruled the night and female fertility, and also served as a calendar, indicating the proper times to reap and sow. On a more esoteric level, it was the moon that bestowed power through dreams and visions.

Many *tribes* determined their ceremonial lives by the lunar calendar. An example of this can be seen in *Sun Bear*'s Earth Astrology, which is in keeping with the tradition of the *Chippewa*. He states in his book *The Medicine Wheel: Earth Astrology*: 'The moon or month during which you were born determines your starting place on the Medicine Wheel and your beginning totem in the mineral, plant, and animal kingdoms.'

According to Earth Astrology, the moons of the year fall under the auspices of the Spirit Keepers of the *Four Directions*. *Waboose*, the Spirit Keeper of the North, presides over the Earth Renewal Moon, the Rest and Cleansing Moon, and the Big Winds Moon. These signal a time for rest and renewal, a time to contemplate the growth of the previous year and prepare for the growth of the year to come.

Following the moons of Waboose are those of *Wabun*, Spirit Keeper of the East. These signal a time for illumination, growth and wisdom, as the Earth's children prepare to grow in the proper way. The moons of Wabun are the Budding Trees Moon, the Frogs' Return Moon, and the Cornplanting Moon.

Next are the moons of *Shawnodese*, Spirit Keeper of the South. These are the moons of rapid growth, when all the Earth comes to flower and bears fruit for that year. These moons are the Strong Sun, Ripe Berries, and Harvest.

Finally, there are the moons of *Mudjekeewis*, Spirit Keeper of the West. These moons bring a time for introspection, a time of gathering strength to look within and contemplate the growth and progress made in the preceding seasons. These are the times to prepare for the season of resting and renewing to come. The moons of Mudjekeewis are the Ducks Fly Moon (which begins on 23 September), the Freeze Up Moon and the Long Snows Moon.

The Skidi *Pawnee* considered shells as the sacred symbol of the moon, and read the moon's activities closely in order to predict the weather. For example, if the moon was seen in its crescent stage with the 'horns' pointing upward, the Pawnee knew that it would be a dry month, but if the horns were pointing downward, it indicated a time of much moisture. They called the moon *Spider Woman*.

Mound Builders The so-called 'Mound Builders' were composed of three separate cultures: the Adena, Hopewell and Mississippians. The Adena and Hopewell lived in the Ohio River basin, and the Mississippians, who evolved later, lived in the Southeast and along the Mississippi River. Their ancient civilizations lasted for some 2,500 years.

The Mound Builders are best remembered for their earthworks, including pyramids, burial mounds, and unique earth effigies. It is assumed that most of the earthworks served ceremonial purposes.

Little is known about the Mound Builders themselves. Where they came from and where they went or why they left remains a mystery, but it is thought that they were nomadic game-hunters who, due to climatic changes, evolved into agriculturists. However, the Adena and Hopewell burial mounds, some of which have been excavated, have revealed weapons, pottery and other artefacts, proving that their culture had a sophisticated knowledge of astronomy and agriculture, as well as art, crafts, religion and social structure. Their jewelry and clothing were exquisite and their trade routes seem to have extended as far south as the Gulf of Mexico. Due to their practice of building burial mounds, some historians have considered the Mound Builders to be 'death cults', although this has become an unpopular theory.

The Adena and Hopewell also built huge earthworks, the most famous of which is the *Serpent Mound* in Ohio. Known as 'effigy mounds', these were built in the form of snakes and other animals. Other mounds were designed in various geometrical shapes.

The modern counterparts of the Mound Builders, who moved into the mound areas, speak little about their prehistoric relatives. Only the Choctaw Indians of Mississippi tell of ancestors who came north and went up the great river. Whether or not these ancestors were the Mound Builders is only speculation. Along with the ancient *Anasazi*, Hohokam, Mayans and others, they have fallen forever into the category of 'lost races'.

Mountains Mountains were special places to the Native Americans. Some mountains were considered sacred, either due to some special power that the peak possessed or because it was the home of certain deities that were a part of the Indians' spiritual legacy. Examples of sacred mountains include the San Francisco Peaks in Flagstaff, Arizona, which are sacred to the *Navajo* as the Holy Mountains of the West, and to the *Hopi* as the 'home' of the *kachinas*; *Corn Mountain*, which is sacred to the *Zunis* and a special pilgrimage site; and Mount Taylor, which is special to the Navajo because it is one of the homes of the *Yei*.

Mudheads See *Hopi*, *Kachinas*.

Mudjeleewis Based on *Sun Bear*'s Earth Astrology, Mudjekeewis is the power of the Spirit Keeper of the West, the power of introspection and strength. The season of Mudjekeewis is the autumn, when the growth of summer stops and the Earth's children prepare for their season of renewal. The daily time of Mudjekeewis is the sunset and twilight, when the activity of the day slows down and day's creatures prepare for their time of sleep and renewal. In human life the time of Mudjekeewis is the middle years, when people have found their direction and work strongly to achieve those tasks that they have been given for this lifetime.

Mullein Mullein is a plant related to the figwort. It has coarse, fuzzy leaves and yellow flowers in tall spikes. The leaves are used in *kinnikinic*, a smoking mixture Indians use in the sacred pipe ceremony. Mullein is also smoked by the southwestern people to aid in *healing* stomach problems.

Mystery Dance See *Sun Dance*.

N

Navajoland

Nakani The Nakani were mythological figures to the Indians of the northern forests. They were evil spirits who looked like humans and possessed supernatural powers. The Nakani kidnapped people and either killed them or made them their slaves. Few who were captured ever returned to tell of their experiences, and those who did escape were often driven insane by the horror of their ordeal.

Nambusa Nambusa is a prominent god figure and great helper to the *Chippewa* people. He could best be described as a 'super-hero'— his deeds include opening rivers for safe travel, fighting for the good of his people and bringing them *corn*.

Naming Ceremony The *Hopi* have a uniquely interesting child 'naming' ceremony. For 20 days after the baby's birth, the mother and child stay in a room that is protected from the rays of the *sun*. At the end of this time, the child is presented to the sun, the giver of life, blessed and given several names. One of these names will stay with the child and will be the name used throughout childhood. Later in his or her life, at the time of initiation into the Kachina Society, the child is given an additional name. At the time of final initiation, Hopi men are given their adult names, while the women carry on with their childhood names.

The godmother cares for the mother and child before and after the birth and during the 20 days that follow. Hopi believe that if the child dies during those 20 days, the mother may have the same child again. They say that the spirit of the baby will climb from the grave, enter the parents' home and wait in the ceiling until a chance comes to be born again. Should it be reborn, it is expected to come in the form of the opposite sex.

Nana Nana was an 80-year-old *Apache medicine man* who went on a 600-mile war trail to fight off the Texas Rangers and the U.S. Cavalry.

Navajo Known in early times as Dineh, 'the People', the Navajo are the largest tribe of Native Americans. They live on the largest reservation in North America, located in northeastern Arizona and northwestern New Mexico, and are one of the few Indian *tribes* that have held on to their land.

The Navajo believe that they emerged from the Underworld in the southwest, while anthropologists say that they came from Asia across the Bering Strait through Canada. They are of the Athapascan linguistic stock. Once nomadic, the Navajo finally settled down and began to raise sheep, goats and *horses*. They often raided other *pueblos* and overran the stolen lands, learning farming, *weaving*, various arts and crafts, and some religious practices from their victims.

The Navajo were a warring people who won most of the battles that they fought with the whites, but in a treaty signed at *Canyon de Chelly* in Arizona on 9 September 1849, they made peace with the United States government. At that time some 8,000 Navajo were marched 300 miles across New Mexico and imprisoned at the Bosque Redondo prison for four years. Those that survived did so on extremely meager rations, most of which were already spoiled and/or infested with weevils. A statement in *The Book of the Navajo* by Raymond Friday Locke declares:

> Almost overnight a people with a culture far in advance of that of any of their neighbors was turned into a nation of beggars, living in the open and eating coffee beans and raw flour to stay alive. Their gods, they said, had deserted them.

Eventually, the Navajo were returned to their homeland, mainly because the government did not know what else to do with them. Home once again, the Indians began to slowly recover from their nightmare of pain and suffering. In the main, they resisted the temptation to attack those who had caused them their trouble and lived within the boundaries of the peace treaty that they had signed with the United States. However there were uprisings from time to

time which frightened the whites and resulted in the final defeat of
the Navajo by Colonel 'Kit' Carson, who attacked them in 1863,
killed most of their sheep and starved them into submission.

Today, the Navajo live on their huge reservation that encompasses
about 24,000 square miles of semi-arid land. Navajo women weave
beautiful *blankets*, and all of their weaving is highly sought-after.
They dress in long, full skirts and loose blouses of bright-colored
velveteen. The men make silver and *turquoise* jewelry and often wear
their hair long and wrapped into a roll in the back of the neck with
a white cotton tie. They live in round houses called *hogans* and on
many parts of the reservation they continue to be sheepherders,
growing the sheep for food and for their wool for weaving. Some
elements within the tribal government are into big business,
including arts and crafts, power plants, gas, oil, timber, parks,
campgrounds and picnic grounds. The largest recreation area that
they run is located at Lake Powell on the Arizona/Utah border. The
lake there was formed by filling Glen Canyon with water, and the
Glen Canyon Dam is one of the largest producers of electric power
in the Southwest, and makes a great deal of money for the tribe.

Navajo Emergence Myth The Navajo Indians believe that when the
first people emerged from the Underworld they needed more light.
So they decided to make a *sun*. They took a large slab of quartz *crystal*
and fashioned it into two disks. The first disk they gave a mask of blue
turquoise that would radiate light and heat. Red coral was placed
around the rim, and *feathers* from the cardinal, *flicker*, lark and *eagle*
were attached to spread the light and heat in all *Four Directions*. The
first disk was then attached to the eastern sky with bolts of lightning.
The second disk, made of ice with a rainbow around it, was also
placed in the sky and became the *moon*. The two disks were given life
by the spirits of two old men who willingly gave their life force to the
sun and moon. The spirit of the moon was *White Shell Man*.

Navajo Night Chant See *Yei-bi-chai*.

New-Life Lodge See *Sun Dance*.

Nez Perce The Nez Perce are the largest group of the Shahaptian
linguistic stock and are related to the Yakima, Umatilla, Walla-Walla,
Cayuse and Palouse Indians. Known as the 'People of the Mountains', they lived in central and western Idaho, northeastern Oregon
and southeastern Washington state. They roamed from the Blue
Mountains of Oregon to the Bitterroot Range of Idaho and Montana
and, during hunting trips, they crossed the Great Continental Divide
and ventured as far east as the Missouri River. They were a skillful
and resourceful people who made deerskin shirts and breechcloths

and tailored *moccasins* and leggings. They carried themselves with great pride and dignity, and many of them wore *blankets* and *feathers*.

Originally the Nez Perce were fishermen and gatherers, but from the 1700s onwards they were horse Indians. The people were not expert agriculturists, their *food* staples being roots, berries and salmon, but they grew camas plants and prepared and used them in a variety of ways. The arrival of *horses* turned them into *buffalo* hunters. Each year they crossed the Rockies on the seasonal hunt on the northern Plains. They elected many hunting chiefs and the younger men joined in forming larger bands which began the evolution of a primal tribal government.

In the early 1800s the Lewis and Clark Expedition reached Nez Perce country. The Indians welcomed them and gave them dried and smoked salmon and roasted camas roots to eat. They also helped them build dugout *canoes* for their trip down the Snake River en route to the Columbia River, and kept their horses for them until they returned when the expedition was completed. They remained friendly to the whites for 50 years, trading with trappers and fur traders as well as with immigrants who came over the Oregon Trail. By this time they had become expert horse breeders and developed the famous Appaloosas. The whites knew them as traders who knew how to drive a hard bargain.

Beginning in 1855, the United States government made treaties with the Indians, and the Nez Perce gave up some of their lands, with the exception of the Nez Perces in the Walla-Walla Valley, the Lower Band, who refused to do so. They also refused to acknowledge that the other bands could give away any of their lands. By 1869, with the treaty-making continuing, the Indians' land had been cut down to a fraction of its original size. Relations between the whites and the Nez Perce turned sour and resistance grew.

Then gold was found on Nez Perce land, bringing a new wave of immigrants. A mining camp was set up at Lewiston, ravaging the land and bringing murder and theft. After the gold seekers came the land seekers. The pressure split the Nez Perce into three parts: those willing to make a deal with the whites, those willing to compromise, and those who wanted no part of any of it and demanded that the whites leave and no more should be allowed to enter their lands. This faction appealed to the U.S. government, reminding them of the 50 years that the Nez Perce had befriended the whites, but to no avail. The government repudiated its treaties and opened the Valley of the Winding Waters to settlement. The famous Nez Perce chief, *Joseph*, fought long and hard for the rights of his people but was finally overwhelmed. It was the end of the line for the Nez Perce, and the Valley of the Winding Waters was lost forever.

Today the Nez Perce live on their reservation in Idaho. They were once expert basketmakers, *weaving* beautiful cups, bowls and fine storage bags, and they are continuing to earn money from their beadwork and leather goods.

Nitsch, Twylah Grandmother Twylah, as she is affectionately called by her friends, is a Seneca elder and direct descendant of the great chief *Red Jacket*. Known as Yehwehnode, 'She whose Voice Rides on the Wind', by her people, in 1970, along with her mother and three other women, she founded the Seneca Historical Society. The society's interests include relations between whites and Indians, arts and crafts shows, and how to obtain financial aid and government grants.

Before she was born, it was known that Twylah would carry on the sacred teachings, and she is indeed still carrying on that tradition today, teaching Indians and non-Indians alike. The Seneca Historical Society has recently received accreditation from the New York State University for teaching the history of the eastern *tribes*.

In Seneca culture, Twylah says that people knew of their spiritual gifts, and their knowledge was based on color. She has found a system by which individuals may come to know this personal information once again.

Twylah is also the clan mother of the Seneca Wolf Clan. She lives on the Cattaraugus Indian Reservation. Information about her work and teachings may be obtained by writing Twylah Nitsch, 12199 Brant Reservation Road, Irving, New York, 14081.

North Star See *Polaris*.

O

Otter

Oglala See *Sioux*.

Ojibway See *Chippewa*.

Olleros See *Apache*.

One-Horned Priests These sacred priests guard the Underworld from which the *Hopi* people first emerged.

Oneida See *Iroquis*.

Only One, The Great Shaman The legend of Only One, the Great *Shaman*, comes from the Nootka, Kwakiutl, Haida and Tlingit Indians of the Northwest.

The story is of a group of young boys who set off in a canoe to the Cave of Fear. The inside of the cave was dark, but as their eyes became accustomed to it, the boys could see a deep pit in the floor. One of them was lowered into the pit by a cedarwood rope. Hearing a scream, the others quickly drew their companion back up to the surface. He stammered, telling the others that the pit was full of wasps! Another boy, saying that he was not afraid, was lowered into the pit but was badly stung.

Then the third boy was lowered deep into the darkness of the pit. As he reached the depths, he heard a loud sound like thunder. He turned and saw a figure in a doorway. The strange figure wore a painted dancing apron fringed with *deer* hoofs. On his head he wore a head-dress of grizzly *bear* claws filled with *eagle* down. He had at his side a *drum* and a pile of *dance* batons. The young man realized that he was in the presence of the spirit of the cave. Soon a group of shamans entered the room and sat themselves in a *circle* on the floor. They began to sing and shake their *rattles*, and their dance batons kept time to the music. The young man was told by the Great Shaman that he had been chosen to do something that no one else could do— bring the dead back to life! The shaman looked into the boy's eyes and then sat down. Instantly, the room was plunged into darkness and the shamans vanished. The boy tugged on the rope and was pulled from the pit. For four days, he lay unconscious. A loud, frightening, whistling sound that came from his house and no one dared enter. When he awoke, he possessed great powers. He traveled all over the land curing illness, destroying evil spirits and raising the dead.

Onondaga See *Iroquis*.

Osceola Osceola was a half-breed, part Indian and part Scottish. He spent most of his boyhood among the Creek Indians, his mother's people. The Creeks to whom he belonged were called 'Seminoles' by the northern bands, because they had left the northern groups and moved to Florida. Seminole means 'runaway'.

Because his father was part white, Osceola had an English name, Billy Powell. But he was known by his Indian name, meaning 'Black Drink Singer', which was given to him by his tribe. The Black Drink Ceremony was an important part of the Seminole tribal rites. Before a major council meeting their chiefs, or Tustenuggees, would drink great amounts of black drink to purify themselves, and when the warriors prepared for the warpath they drank it too.

The Seminoles tried to get along with the white man, but they were forced onto a reservation totally unfit for habitation and the food and provisions promised them never arrived. So they began to live outside of their reservation. This was in 1825. At the same time slave owners claimed the Seminoles were harboring runaway slaves and sent raiding parties to take them back. These parties often took back not only slaves, but free men and Seminoles as well.

The government's next move was to try and force the removal of all the Seminoles to Oklahoma, or the Indian Territory as it was known then. They sent a delegation of six Seminole chiefs along with interpreters to look at the territory, and because of the suffering the people had had in Florida, they agreed to resettle. However, many of the Seminole people then refused to be moved, contending that these six chiefs had just been a delegation to look at the land and that they were not bound by their decision. Even some of the chiefs who had signed the relocation document now refused, claiming it was a fraud and had been misrepresented to them. But the government would recognize only the chiefs who were in agreement to their treaty, and demanded that all the Indians be removed.

At a meeting of Seminole leaders at Fort King in Georgia, Osceola showed himself a great leader and statesman, speaking out strongly against the removal. After more negotiations, General Clinch, the fort commander, threatened to use troops to force the Indians to move. Osceola was arrested for his refusal to comply, and some of the other chiefs were forced to sign an agreement to relocate. In order to gain his release, Osceola, too, had to sign. Later, however, in council with the other chiefs, he decided to refuse to honor an order obtained in such a way. The chiefs also agreed that any chief who made preparations to relocate would be killed, and executed one there and then.

The Seminoles prepared for battle. Arms were bought wherever possible, and the tribe went into hiding in the swamps. They made hit and run raids against the settlements and soldiers, killing hundreds. The settlers who had led the raids to recapture their slaves and take Indians into slavery were hunted down and killed too. As a result, more slaves fled their masters and joined the Seminoles.

Osceola himself led his men against the Indian agency on the reservation and killed Wiley Thompson, the military general of Georgia, who had forced him to sign the agreement. President Jackson ordered still more troops into the area, but the Seminoles kept out of the way of major troop concentrations and instead hit small outposts and settlements. The soldiers meanwhile suffered from malaria and other sickness; in fact, more died of disease than of conflict with the Indians.

Finally, however, Osceola and his people tired of being chased. Micanopy, the Seminoles' head chief, made an agreement to migrate to the Indian Territory. The Seminoles were to assemble at Tampa Bay. Osceola and his people came in. Osceola had been sick, suffering from malaria, and was very tired and thin. The Seminoles had hardly got into camp before the slave catchers were there, claiming Indians and blacks alike, and neither were offered any protection. Osceola and some other chiefs escaped to their villages, where many of their people still remained, and then Osceola returned, bringing warriors with him. He ordered Micanopy and the other Seminoles to return to hiding in the Everglades. Around 700 Indians joined him. The government blamed the whole thing on the Seminoles and ordered renewed fighting against them. Meanwhile, however, some Seminole bands did relocate, but many of them died along the way from starvation and sickness.

Approximately two years later, in the latter part of 1837, armies were again sent against the Seminoles. Osceola sent word that he wished to talk peace and waited in his camp under a flag of truce. The Americans came to him, but they had 200 armed men following at a distance. They surrounded the camp and Osceola and his people were seized. Public outcry spoke out against this action but the government paid it no mind. Osceola was imprisoned at Fort Moultrie near Charleston, South Carolina, where he again took sick. He was offered a white doctor but refused, asking for a doctor from his own people. However, it was too late. He gathered his loved ones around him and dressed in the way of his people, shook hands with the post officers, bid farewell to his friends and the chiefs of his tribe, then lay back and died. The post doctor cut off his head and preserved it to keep as a souvenir.

Today there are still bands of Seminoles living in Florida, the descendants of those who refused to leave or surrender. It is a beautiful sight to see them still dressing and living in the old way.

Otter Based on *Sun Bear*'s Earth Astrology, the otter is the totem of people born between 20 January and 18 February. Otters are members of the weasel family and range from three to five feet in length and weigh between 35 and 70 pounds. Sea and river otters look very much the same except that the sea otter has a shorter tail and is smaller. The river otter has a chocolate-brown coat with light grey underparts and throat, and the sea otter is a very dark grey with lighter grey undersides. All otters have a voracious appetite, because of their rapid metabolism. They eat fish, shellfish, insects, ducks and rodents. They have the ability to use rocks to open the shellfish, making them one of the few animals that has mastered the art of using tools. Otters also have a wide vocabulary, which consists of chips, squeals, screeches, hiccoughs, chuckles—and hisses when they are angry. Some of their calls carry for more than a mile.

Ouray See *Ute*.

P

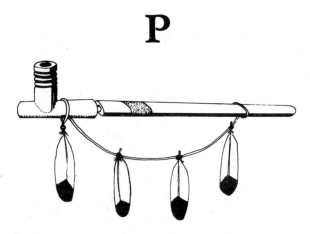

Sacred Pipe

Pahos Pahos are 'prayer *feathers*' or 'prayer sticks' that are made by the *Hopi* Indians. The simplest form of paho is a single down feather from an *eagle* that has been attached to a string of cotton cut the same length as that between the wrist and the tip of the little finger.

One of the most important pahos is the male-and-female paho. It consists of two eight-inch-long red-willow sticks. Sometimes both sticks are painted blue while other times one is painted black. The female stick has a notch on the upper end that is painted brown, symbolizing the female genitals. Binding them together at the base is a small cornhusk sack folded to a point that is symbolic of the spiritual body. Inside, cornmeal representing the physical body is placed, along with a bit of *corn* pollen that symbolizes the power of fertility. There is also a drop of honey to represent the love of the Creator for the people. Both paho sticks are tied together, for the Creator is both male and female, and in mankind both sexes must come together to reproduce. The cotton string that ties them together symbolizes the life cord, while the down feather which is tied to the end of the paho represents the breath of life. A long cord indicates a long life.

Pahos are made in a prayerful manner and are ritually smoked over.

A paho will then be taken to a sacred shrine where it is stuck in the rocks, tied to a bush or placed in a cleft until its energy has spread to, and been absorbed by, the forces of life to which the prayers have been dedicated.

Pahotakawa The Skidi band of the *Pawnee* Indians have a myth called Meteor's Child. It tells of a time before the stars fell to Earth, when there was a being in the land known as Pahotakawa, meaning 'Kneeprint-by-the-Water'. He had come to the Pawnee people from the sky as a *meteorite* and would spend time with them. He eventually became a star in the northern sky, the village patron star. He was always ready to give to the people. Once he told them that something wonderful was going to take place in the heavens and that they should not be afraid, for it would not signal the end of the world. He said that a large meteor would fall on the plain and that it would be in the shape of a turtle. In its fall, it would cause other meteors to light up and fly through the sky.

Many years later, near the Platte River, while the people were in their *tipis*, the meteors came. The Indians remembered the words of Pahotakawa. They went out and tried to catch the meteors that were flying around like birds. Two or three years later, the men were on a *buffalo* hunt when they came across a barren place, where no grass grew. Puzzled, the men wondered why this was so. It was a smooth, round place with a stone of many colors sticking out of the center. When they dug it out, they found that it was shaped like a turtle! Their leader, Chief Big-Eagle, reminded them of the meteor that Pahotakawa had promised, so they placed it on a pony and took it into the village. The people offered *tobacco* and smoke to it. The priests were sent for and they made pipe to it. From then on, the meteor was carried wherever the people went, for they believed that it was part of the Morning Star. When the Skidi moved out of Nebraska into Oklahoma, they placed it on a high hill in the western part of the state, where it disappeared, stolen, it is believed, by whites.

The meteor was said to have great powers. Before battle, warriors would go to it to pray and offer smoke to it. They also believed that the stone kept disease away.

Painted Cave Painted Cave is located near San Marcos Pass in Santa Barbara, California. It is the site of wonderful multi-colored rock paintings drawn by the ancient *Chumash* Indians, who created the finest rock art in North America. Archeologists believe that the paintings were done by *shamans* who used or created them as a part of their magical rituals. The paintings may also have been inspired by hallucinogenic visions. Their meaning remains unknown.

Palolokon See *Water Serpent Ceremony.*

Papago The Papago call themselves the 'Bean People' and live in the southwestern United States of America. They are closely related to the *Pima* people of the same area. Both are believed to be descendants of the Hohokam, an ancient tribe of the area.

The Papago are agriculturists who irrigate their desert land by flooding. They have always had to defend themselves against the neighboring *Apaches*. The women are known for their *baskets* woven from yucca fiber. Their traditional houses are round and flat-topped and usually have a brush ramada attached to them, that is, a roof made of twigs or branches added on to the house to provide shade. The Papago now live on a reservation of about three million acres in Arizona.

Parker, Quanah Quanah Parker belonged to a band of *Comanche* known as Kwahadi, meaning 'Antelope-Eaters'. His mother was Cynthia Ann Parker, a white woman who had been captured, together with four others, in a Comanche raid on Parker's Fort on 19 May 1836, when she was nine years old. Nakoni, the Comanche chief, later took her as his wife. The Comanches were polygamists, so Quanah had many half-sisters and brothers.

When Quanah grew to manhood, he became a great leader of his people. He is credited with bringing the peyote religion to his people and practicing it faithfully. In 1867, when the other Comanche bands made a treaty with the United States at Medicine Lodge and went to a reservation, he refused, and led his people out on the Staked Plains. He hunted *buffalo* and antelope where he chose, for this was the land of his people. When the white buffalo hunters and Texas Rangers pressed close, he fought back, and his warriors raided all over Mexico and Texas. But as band after band of Comanches went to the reservation, Quanah saw that the old life was over.

In 1875, a group of government peacemakers came in search of Quanah Parker. He listened to their treaty talk but not all of it was to his liking. To be forced to live in one place on a reservation, and to have to ask someone for permission to do something was contrary to his free nature. But he wanted peace for his people. He was tired of having the Texas Rangers hunt them like wild animals. Therefore, on 2 June 1875, Quanah Parker rode in at the head of his band, consisting of 100 warriors, 300 women, children and elders, and 1,500 horses. At Fort Sill, then Indian Territory, he gave up his arms and pledged his people to the ways of peace.

Then Quanah set about learning the ways of the white man. If his people must live with the whites, he would lead them in their ways. He built a white man's house and went into ranching, encouraging his people to do so as well. He counseled his people in learning from the white man, and fought to protect their rights. If he felt his people had been cheated or suffered injustice at the hand of the white man, he was there to speak for them. Yet if they did wrong, he would turn them over to the white man's law. From that time onwards he wore the white man's clothing except at special ceremonial times, when he put back on his Indian clothes.

He was a man of great integrity. Once he had placed his foot on the path of peace, he never turned back. His word was a bond. In Texas there is a town that proudly bears the name of Quanah, in his honor.

The inscription on his tombstone reads: 'Resting here until day breaks, and shadows fall, and darkness disappears is Quanah Parker: last chief of the Comanches.'

Parukati See *Bright Star*.

Pawnee The Pawnee tribe was part of the Caddoan family, which consisted of a federation of *tribes* that lived along the Platte River in what is now the state of Nebraska. The Pawnee lived in *earth lodges*. Their major crop was *corn* and they hunted *buffalo* and other game. In the old days, the Pawnees would wear their hair in a horn-like coil called a 'pariki'. They called themselves 'Men of Men'.

The Pawnees made *medicine* bundles that were a sacred trust to each village in the federation. They believed that all they needed, including themselves, had come from the sky. They also had secret societies that were founded upon the powers of supernatural animal spirits.

The Pawnees lost much of their tribe due to disease brought by the white man. They served as Indian scouts during the Indian Plains wars in the late 1820s and early 1830s. Afterwards, many of them were relocated to Indian Territory in Oklahoma, where they settled with the *Ponca* and Oto people.

Pawnee Bear Society The Skidi band of the *Pawnee* symbolized the Creator by the *bear*, who received his powers from the *sun*. Bears were painted on their *tipis* for protection. Members of the Pawnee Bear Society, called Bear Warriors, held *ceremonies* for the power of victory. The leader wore symbols of Mother Corn, the Evening Star, Father Hawk and the Morning Star, and prayed for protection and success in battle.

Pawnee Star Chart The Pawnee Star Chart was a replica of the northern hemisphere that was painted on a *buckskin* in at least three different pigments. The chart shows most of the important constellations identified by the *Pawnee* and is believed to be about a hundred years old. Originally it was kept in one of the sacred *medicine* bundles that the Indians believed had been given to them by the star gods. The Star Chart is now on display in the Field Museum in Chicago.

Peacemaker League Founded by a spiritual leader of the *Iroquis* Indians, the Peacemaker League was held to be responsible for introducing peace to the world. The League led to the founding of the original Six Nations Iroquis Confederacy, which is the same as the *Iroquis League of Six Nations*.

Penobscot The Penobscots, whose name means 'It Flows on the Rocks', are of Albonquin stock and were once a powerful tribe who lived in what is now New England. They belonged to the Abnaki confederacy, which included the Malecites and Passamaquaddies. They were canoeists and fishermen who also made shell *wampum* and *pipes*, and did fine beading and *quillwork*. They were known to be hospitable, peaceful Indians. Today, the Penobscots live on the Indian Island Reservation at Old Town, Maine.

Peters, John See *Slow Turtle*.

Petroglyphs Petroglyphs are ancient drawings that were done on rocks, cave walls and ceilings, and cliffs by various Indian people. Some of the most famous include the star ceilings in *Canyon de Chelly* in Arizona, *Painted Cave* in Santa Barbara, California, and the *Anasazi* ruins in *Chaco Canyon*, New Mexico.

Some of the drawings seem to tell a story and/or speak of events that occurred to the ancient people, while others indicate the appearance of shooting stars and comets, the phases of the *moon*, the eclipses of the *sun* and moon, and other celestial phenomena. In a manner of speaking, petroglyphs were the first *language* of 'the Ancient Ones'.

Peyote See *Mescal*.

King Philip Sometimes called Metacom, King Philip was the youngest son of Massasoit, chief of the Wampanoag. He became chief after the death of his older brother, Alexander, who died at the hands of the Plymouth colonists. In spite of this, Philip pledged himself to the peace that his father had made with the colony. However, in 1671, the English started trespassing on Philip's hunting grounds. Their continual disregard for the rights of the Indians and encroachment upon their lands resulted in a war known as the King Philip War.

Through his efforts and energy, King Philip was able to induce many other *tribes* to join with his own people in battle against the colonists. He had a force of 600 men of his own, and formed an alliance with the powerful Narragansetts, the Nipmucks of Connecticut and the Indians of Maine. The war was fought in 1675 and 1676. Philip traveled all over the frontier, exhorting and encouraging tribes to fight for the Indian race as a whole. He showed great courage and skill at all times, and when he finally lost to the English, it was only due to their superior arms and manpower. In all his warfare, he never mistreated any captives, although the English were torturing and hanging his people and even selling them into slavery abroad.

King Philip was finally cornered in a swamp and shot by soldiers under a military man named Church. After his death, rather than giving him a decent burial, the English had him quartered. His head was carried to Plymouth Colony to be displayed at the colonists' Thanksgiving feast, and his only son, a boy of nine, was sold into slavery.

Piegans See *Blackfeet*.

Piki Piki, made from blue cornmeal, is the sacred ceremonial bread made by the *Hopi* and other southwestern *pueblo* peoples. The batter is made from blue cornmeal mixed with water and a pinch of juniper ash. It is then poured onto a hot rock to cook. This takes very little time, and while the piki is still hot it is rolled into a cylindrical shape and left to cool. Piki is eaten during *ceremonies* and on special social occasions.

Pima The Pima are Indians of the Uto-Aztecan linguistic family who live in southern Arizona near the Gila and Salt Rivers. These people farm the land, growing *corn*, *beans*, squash, cotton and *tobacco*. Like the *Papago*, they have a sophisticated irrigation system, most likely learned from the ancestral Hohokam. The Pima are also excellent basketmakers. The women fashion *baskets* of all sizes and shapes, some from yucca fiber and some miniature ones made from horsehair. Most of the Pima people now live on the Gila River Reservation in Arizona.

Pipes Many *tribes* of Indian people used the pipe both as a smoking tool and as a sacred ceremonial tool. The smoke is a sacred offering to the spirits and the pipe itself is a 'telephone line' to the *Great Spirit*. The pipe is used for making prayers and the smoke carries their message to the Great Spirit.

Each tribe had its own type of pipe. Some were fashioned out of wood, some of bone, while others were made from slate, sandstone, catlinite (red pipestone), quartzite or clay. All Indians believed the pipe to be a gift from divine beings, differing with each tribe. *Tobacco* and other smoking mixtures were burned in the bowl of the pipe, which was like an altar. Since ancient times some pipes have been carved into the shapes of various animals. Some of the bowls are disk-shaped, others flat with a wooden stem. The pipe stems were usually separate from the bowl but when the two were united, the pipe became sacred. Stems were made from various types of wood, usually ash and sumac, and the wood was split, grooved and glued together to form a tube. The core of the stem was burned out so that smoke could be drawn through easily.

The *Sioux* believed that the pipe was a gift to the people from one of their deities, White Buffalo Calf Woman. The Sioux calumet, sometimes known as the 'Grand Pipe', was about two or three feet in length and had a stem of ash decorated with *beads* and *feathers*. The whole calumet was painted with sacred symbols. Sometimes the pipe bowls were ringed, representing the *four directions* and/or the four winds. The calumet was smoked only on special occasions such as to settle quarrels or during the signing of treaties, which is probably where the term 'peace pipe' originated.

The pipe was, and still is, at the heart of Indian ceremonial life. However, there were also pipes that were used for pleasure, the most popular being the so-called 'elbow' pipe, sometimes called the 'squaw pipe' by the whites, for women smoked them too. Pipes were also connected to the Indians' *medicine* work and *healing*. A special 'medicine tobacco' was grown by some *tribes*, that is, grown and harvested in a ceremonial manner. The pipe was often smoked at the time of death, as a form of last rites.

Pleiades The Pleiades were sacred to many *tribes* of Native people and there are many legends associated with them.

One such story comes from the *Kiowa*, and tells of their *emergence* from a hollow log. One day, eight Kiowa children, seven girls and a boy, were playing and, while pretending to be a *bear*, the boy actually turned into one! He began to run on all fours and was covered with fur. Claws replaced his fingers. He let out a great roar, causing the girls to run faster and faster to escape him. Suddenly, a voice called to the girls, saying, 'Come up here!' The girls looked up but saw only trees. They realized that the voice had come from a giant tree stump. They jumped on the stump and it began to rise upward. The bear tried to reach them but they were too high. The girls continued to rise upward into the sky and became the Pleiades.

Plenty Coups Plenty Coups was a powerful chief of the Montana *Crows* in the early 1800s. His achievements were so great that his bonnet and its feathered trailer extended all the way to the ground. This attested to his greatness because the number of *feathers* indicated that his prowess in battle had been outstanding, to earn him so many. His tribe said that because he was so great a man, they would pay him the highest honor: they would never have another chief after him. This was not uncommon in that some *tribes* would simply have a 'ceremonial' chief, an honorary title which did not necessarily hold any political or religious power.

Pocohontas See *Powhatan*.

Polaris Polaris, the North Star, was known as the 'Chief Star' and 'The Star That Does Not Walk Around' by the Skidi *Pawnees*. It was the most important of all the stars who watched over the band in the heavens. Polaris directed their motions and made certain that none of them lost their way. To some degree, the North Star represented *Tirawahat*, the Creator, because it did not move, showing its immortality. The North Star also controlled the north winds and snowstorms. The North Star *medicine* bundle was supposed to have belonged to the chiefs of the various villages within the Pawnee Federation and been given to the Skidi by the first chief who knew how to use it properly.

Ponca As part of the *Sioux* tribe, the Poncas are closely related to the Osage, Kansa and Omaha Indians, who lived in *earth lodges* near Lake Andes, South Dakota. They grew *corn*, hunted *buffalo*, and adopted many of the *ceremonies* of the Plains Indians, including the *Sun Dance* and the sacred pipe.

The Sioux had always fought the Ponca for territorial rights, even though the Ponca were friendly towards them and formed part of the same tribe. They were greatly diminished by smallpox and other diseases brought by the whites, and finally, because of their fighting with the Sioux, they were forced to surrender their land to the Sioux and were removed to Indian Territory where most of them died.

Chief Pontiac Pontiac was an Ottawa Indian, a natural-born leader who lived in the mid-eighteenth century. The arrogance of the British settlers troubled him; he felt that they were not as friendly and willing to get along with the Indians as the French. The British had allowed their settlers to push beyond the boundaries set by the various *tribes*, and appeals to remove them were not accepted either by the Crown or by its local governors. Also the French had given the Indians guns and ammunition and provisions for their hunting, and French traders would come to the Indian camps and give them supplies instead of making the Indians travel long distances to different trading posts. But after the defeat of the French by the British, everything changed, and it is said that the proud British treated the Indians like dirt in their own lands.

Pontiac decided to unite all the tribes against the British. So he traveled from tribe to tribe with the *wampum* belt of war, asking the Indians to take up the hatchet against the British. He was a tremendous orator, and when they found out that he was going to speak, the tribes came from all over to hear him. Pontiac reminded them of the wrongs they had suffered at the hands of the British, and had a way of stirring the people. Where he could not go personally, the chiefs who had heard him would take up his cry.

Gradually, Chief Pontiac built his armies across thousands of miles of wilderness lands. His attack was not composed of simple hit and run raids, but was rather an organized, perfectly-timed action. The league of tribes stretched from the east coast all the way to present-day Minnesota and Iowa and down to Choctaw country, and included the Ottawa, *Chippewa*, Sauk, Fox, Winnebago, Miami, Wea, Kashaskia, Mascouten, Piankashow, Kickapoo, Shawnee, Delaware, Poawatomi and Hurons. Even though most of these tribes are enemies, they put aside their differences to fight in the Pontiac confederacy against the British.

However, after France made peace with Britain, with little or no provisions to carry on the fight, one by one the tribes left Chief Pontiac, made their separate peace with the British and went on with their lives. This ended Pontiac's dream of driving out the invaders and returning the land to the Indians. He tried to rally the tribes for the following two years, but to no avail, for the British bought the chiefs of the tribes with trade goods or cowed them with treats of troops. Finally, in April 1769, Pontiac was killed by a jealous Indian for reasons that remain unexplained. However, he is remembered in history as a man who shook the British Lion and fought hard for his people and the things he valued and believed in.

Potlatch See *Tribes*.

Powam See *Bean Dance*.

Powhatan In 1584 Sir Walter Ralegh arrived in Virginia and spoke of the natives as peaceful and friendly, and to quote, 'a more kind loving people could not be.' He carried on trade and barter with them. Sir Richard Grenville visited the area the next year and left over a hundred men to form the colony of Roanoke. While on an exploration trip in the surrounding country, they tried to lay the groundwork for future relations with the Indians, although from the very beginning relations between Indians and whites were never friendly for long.

Soon afterwards, Captain John Smith arrived and, with his followers, set up Jamestown Colony—an undertaking for which they were completely unsuitable. These were gamblers, spendthrifts and people who had never worked in their lives and didn't intend to. In their opinion, the 'New World', as they called it, was a place full of rich Indian *tribes* from whom you just stole gold. (Up to that time the Spanish had been very successful at taking gold in South America.) So with Smith's men not willing to or capable of work, the colony started off in bad shape.

The colonists took to trading with the Indians with hatchets, *beads*, and copper. The Indians were reluctant to trade at first, but after the colonists threatened to destroy their village and winter *corn* supply and kill a few of the people, they agreed to sell corn to the colony for trade goods.

In an incident during which Captain Smith was taken captive by the Indians, he was taken to the court of Powhatan. Powhatan at this time ruled like a monarch from his capital at Werowocomoco. Thirty tribes were subject to his rule, but he ruled by consent of the governed. He is described as a strong, powerfully-built man of 60, a noble figure. He is referred to as a king by the colonists. In fact King James I of England decided that since Powhatan was a native king, he should be crowned, and so he sent a crown, scarlet cloak and many other presents, including a bed and furniture set. Captain Smith and a man named Newport were to do the honors. They set out for Powhatan's village. They had a hard time getting him to kneel, but finally one man leaned on him to get him to stoop a little and, with the help of three others, they crowned him and fired their muskets in salute. This startled Powhatan and, for a moment, he felt he was about to be attacked. But all was well.

After this, however, Powhatan cautioned his tribes about dealing with the whites. He felt that they were increasing in strength too much, and that they were also cheating the natives. However, Captain Smith made another visit in the winter of 1608, taking along 46 men and a small ship with two barges with goods to trade. After some dispute they completed the trade—but not to the Indians' satisfaction, as threats of force were used. From then on there was constant distrust between Powhatan's people and the English colonists.

After Captain Smith returned to England, Powhatan's people became even more hostile toward the colonists, and if it had not been for the efforts of Powhatan's daughter, Pocohontas, they might have run the colonists out of the country. Powhatan finally made a sort of peace with the British after Pocohontas married a young man named John Rolfe. She went to England at a later date and there she died.

Prayer Feathers See *Pahos*.

Prayer Sticks See *Pahos*.

Prayer Ties Prayer ties are made by wrapping a small amount of *tobacco* in a three inch square of cotton cloth of one of four colors that represent the *four directions* and the four Spirit Keepers: red, yellow, black (or blue), and white. While the prayer tie is being made, prayers for any special purpose are placed into it. Prayer ties are used in the Sweat Ceremony (see *Inipi*), in the building of the modern *medicine wheel*, or for personal *ceremonies* and, as a rule, are burned afterwards, the smoke carrying the prayer to the *Great Spirit*.

Pueblo An Indian village. Indian villages were concentrated settlements, usually consisting of inhabitants from one specific tribe or band within a given tribe. Villages consisted of ceremonial grounds or sites, dwellings (in the form of *earth lodges*, wickiups, *tipis*, or *hogans*) and, oftentimes, burial grounds. The village was often situated near a reliable water source and was in a place that was easily defended and protected. Each village had a leader, male as a rule. The leader could be a chief and/or a *medicine man*, and he took care of the charge of the political, ceremonial and social affairs of the people.

Villages could change seasonally if the tribe involved was a tribe of nomadic hunters, such as the *buffalo* hunters.

Q

Quetzalcoatl Temple Relief *c.*10 AD

Quarter Stars The Skidi *Pawnee* people honored four bright stars which they believed had special powers and were the 'Pillars of Heaven'. Although it is uncertain precisely which stars they were, it is known that the Indians gave the four stars certain attributes and assigned each of them to one of the semi-cardinal directions.

The first star was the feminine Star of the Northwest. It corresponded to the spring season, lightning, the color yellow, the setting *sun*, yellow *corn*, and children. Its totem was the mountain lion.

The second was the male Red Star of the Southeast. It corresponded to the dawn, young people, the summer season, clouds and red corn, and was considered brother to the Morning Star. Its totem was the wolf.

The third was the female White Star of the Southwest. It corresponded to the winter, old age, the wind, *moon*, and white corn. Its totem was the wildcat.

Finally, there was the Big Black Meteorite Star of the Northeast, which corresponded to the night, black clouds and thunder, and black corn. It is said that this star gave animals the power to communicate with people. Its totem was the black *bear*.

Quetzalcoatl Quetzalcoatl is most widely known as the feathered serpent god of the Mayans. He is said to have lived as a human male around 940–1070 AD, although there is disagreement among various writers. There are suggestions that he traveled as far as Yucatan, the land of the Mayans, and to Oaxaca, the land of the Zapotecs, as well as throughout the Great Valley of Mexico. At Teotihuacan in south central Mexico, there are ancient wall carvings that depict a man carrying the quetzal *feathers* and snake that symbolize Quetzalcoatl. In ancient Mexico 'Feathered Serpent' meant 'The Lord of the Dawn'. Legends suggest that a human being would come at different times, appearing in different bodies and characters, but bringing the same message of hope and peace as Quetzalcoatl. Quetzalcoatl promised that one day he would return to the people. This prophecy is generally believed to mean that there would be the return of some wonderful sacred teaching, not necessarily the return of the person who was once Quetzalcoatl.

Quillwork Porcupine quills are used by many Indian *tribes* in various crafts, such as beading and other decorative work. The hollow quills are often threaded and strung like *beads* on ear-rings, necklaces and bracelets. Quills can also be pressed flat and glued onto sacred objects, and lend themselves well to paint and dye.

R

Rattle

Rattles Rattles are used in rituals to help inspire the participants. They also aid in keeping the rhythm during sacred *dance*s, as well as inspiring the dancers themselves and adding interest for the spectators. There are several different types of rattle and they are made from many materials. Rattles can be filled with various noise-makers, depending upon the sound desired, including seeds, pebbles, buckshot and shells. The most common rattles are made from *gourds* and contain gourd seeds. The neck of the gourd serves as a handle. These rattles are very easy to make and possess strong *medicine*. *Chippewa* rattles have *corn* kernels or wild rice grains inside. The *Cherokee* and other southern *tribes* put Indian wheat inside, producing another sound entirely. Seeds inside a rattle were considered a necessity for they gave the rattle potency.

Dance rattles are made in two ways. One way is for the rattle to be left hollow and the filling to be placed inside. In the other, the rattling devices are attached to the outside. Gourd rattles are mostly used by the southwestern, southern, Plains and Californian Indians, as well as by the woodland Indians of the north and east.

Rawhide See *Buckskin*.

Raven The raven is sacred to the *Eskimos* and respected by many other *tribes*. The Eskimos believe that in the beginning a raven was born of the darkness. He was weak and small and his magical powers, which he did not know he had, were not yet developed. He began to search around to determine where he was and after feeling the water, grass, and trees, he pondered on them, on what made them grow and on who he was. He soon realized that he was Tulugaukuk, the Raven Father, the Creator of All Life. As he flew down through the darkness he found a new land. He called it Earth. Raven brought it to life and covered it with growing things.

One day, while surveying his Earth, he noticed a giant peapod, out of which fell a man, the first Eskimo. Raven fed the man and created two animals, the musk-ox and the caribou, for him to eat. He told the man to always treat the animals with respect. For days Raven continued creating other animals and, finally, he created a woman to be a companion for the man. He taught the man to build a house and a canoe, and how to sew skins for clothes. Soon the first Eskimo and his wife became parents. Three other men then fell from the peapods and Raven taught them as before. Soon there were many children.

However, the people disobeyed Raven. They killed more animals than necessary and paid no attention to Raven, who decided therefore to return to the Sky Land, causing darkness to cover the Earth once again. From time to time, however, he allowed the *sun* to peep through, providing enough light for the people to hunt.

In Sky Land, Raven took a *snow goose* for a wife. They had a son called Raven Boy. One day, while Raven slept, Raven Boy crept into the chest where the sun was stored and soared into the darkness, carrying it with him. Raven flew after Raven Boy, begging him to come back and not hide the sun forever. Raven Boy, hearing his father's words, set the sun back in its place so that light could return to the Earth once again. With a flip of his wing, Raven Boy sent the sky spinning around the Earth, carrying the sun with it and creating day and night. This was done so that the people would not forget the evils of darkness.

The raven is representative of the zodiacal sign of Libra in *Sun Bear*'s Earth Astrology.

Raven Boy See *Raven*.

Red Cloud Red Cloud belonged to the Oglala Division of the Teton *Sioux*. For years his people had been driving white invaders from their country, when in 1866 the federal government asked for a peace council with the Sioux to be held at Fort Laramie. But, at the same time, the government had ordered Colonel Henry Carrington to the

Powder River country where he was to construct forts along the Bozeman Trail. These forts, deep in Sioux territory, would have been a direct violation of their rights, setting the whites up to break any treaty agreement before it was even signed. Red Cloud saw the colonel there with his men, and became angry, saying that he wanted nothing to do with any 'smog-producing engine' (locomotive) going through his land and driving off game. Thereupon he left the peace council.

In July 1866, Colonel Carrington once more encroached onto Sioux territory, choosing a site there for the construction of Fort Phil Kearney. Red Cloud assembled his warriors and began harassing the troops. Whenever a detail left the main body, they were attacked. This began several years of fighting. In spite of much loss of life, Red Cloud was able to keep the Sioux interested in holding out to protect themselves and their lands. Finally, the United States asked for another peace council. Red Cloud demanded they leave all their forts and get out of Sioux country, for there could be no peace as long as they remained. Only when the troops had been withdrawn would he sign the treaty. The soldiers pulled down their flag and left their forts, which were immediately set on *fire* by the Indians. This was the last fighting that Red Cloud ever did. He lived on, victorious, among his people, a great counselor and source of wisdom.

Today Red Cloud's grandson and great-grandson live in Rapid City, South Dakota. They take great pride in their heritage, are good Indian dancers and know much of their history.

Red Hawk Based on *Sun Bear*'s Earth Astrology, the red hawk is the totem of people born between 21 March and 19 April. It has a broad wing span and a fan-shaped tail. The adult is the only hawk with a red tail. It is a large hawk, often two feet long with a wing span of up to four and a half feet. When these hawks are immature, they have a brown body and underparts streaked with brown. Their tail is brown above and barred with brown below, only becoming red as they mature. In adult hawks the chest, throat and stomach are usually white streaked with brown.

These hawks are magnificent in flight, soaring and circling for long periods, and sometimes twisting their tail at an angle to their body. They can also be real acrobats, especially when they are mating. They can touch their mates in midair or drop several thousand feet in one dive.

Red Jacket Red Jacket, Grandfather to *Twylah Nitsch*, was a great Seneca chief who was a staunch defender of his people and their traditions in the late 1800s. He was also said to have been a magnificent orator.

Red Ocher Red ocher is a natural mineral pigment that was used as a dye and for painting objects.

Roach See *Grass Dance.*

Roadman A roadman is a peyote priest of the Native American Church who travels from place to place presiding over sacred peyote *ceremonies.*

Rolling Thunder Rolling Thunder is a *medicine man* and spiritual leader, philosopher, and spokesman for the *Cherokee* and *Shoshone* Indian *tribes.* He has been a speaker at many conferences throughout the world and currently resides in Carlin, Nevada. Rolling Thunder is deeply involved with the rights of the Native peoples of North America.

Roman Nose Roman Nose was a *Cheyenne* chief who fought bravely for his people, driving off hunters who came to slaughter the *buffalo* for their hides. His name was given to him by the whites, who said that he had a proud, hawk-like face. He always rode into battle wearing a long war bonnet decorated with *eagle feathers*, each of which stood for a brave deed against the enemy.

Roman Nose is said to have possessed a magical stone that was powerful war *medicine.* He wore it tied to his hair, at the back of his head. Before battle, the chief would sprinkle his clothing with sacred gopher dust and paint his horse with hailstone patterns. A curious thing is told about Roman Nose's medicine: he could eat or cook with no metal, only wood or earthenware. This is believed to have brought about his death, for he broke his own rule just before going into battle at Beecher Island by eating buffalo that had been cooked in a metal pot and eating it with a metal knife and spoon.

Ross, John John Ross was a *Cherokee* who worked to save his people from removal to Indian Territory, and then worked to protect them while 18,000 were being removed on what is now called the *Trail of Tears.*

S

Sun Bear

Sacred Site A sacred site is a place that is respected by the Indians, either because it has some special power or because it was the site of a great battle or vision, or because it is the site of a spiritual object or event. A sacred site might be a mountain that is of some significance to a tribe, or a spring, a hill or the place where a special rock, cave, tree or canyon existed. Ceremonial sites are also considered sacred.

Sage Sage is a herb that is held sacred by most Indian people. Besides being used as an ingredient in *kinnikinic*, it is burned and its smoke used for cleansing the body and the aura prior to *ceremonies*, as well as for cleansing *medicine* objects of any negative energy before use.

Sakajawea In 1800, a raiding band of *Crows* captured a *Shoshone* girl whose name was Sakajawea. She was taken east and sold to the Mandans on the Missouri River. She married a French fur trapper, Toussaint Charbonneau, when she was 18 years old and had a baby. She remained captive, however, until Lewis and Clark came through. They needed an interpreter and a guide for their expedition to lead them to the distant sea, and Sakajawea's husband struck a deal for her to go.

Sakajawea led them with her baby strapped to her back. She remembered the country that she had not seen since her childhood, and recognized landmarks from her journey after being captured some six years before. She danced with joy when the expedition reached Shoshone country and she was reunited with her people, but she chose to go on with Lewis and Clark, and guided them through the Rocky Mountains and down to the coast where they spent the winter, before returning with them in the spring to her Shosone people.

Sandpainting Sandpainting is a form of spiritual art that is used by most *tribes* of the Southwest. Over time, it has evolved into a highly complex art form, and there can be as many as a thousand designs incorporated into a single painting made from various colors of sand.

The *Navajo* make the most prominent use of this art, for it is a major part of their *healing* rituals. The Navajo priest, known as a 'chanter' or 'singer', leads the rites and, along with his assistants, uses the powdered pigments to draw a design on the desert floor. At the end of the rite, the priest takes dust from various parts of the bodies of the deities in the sandpainting and applies it to the body of the sick person.

Sans Arcs See *Sioux*.

Chief Seattle Chief Seattle was the chief of the Suquamish and Duwamish Indians. He was born near the present city in Washington state that is named after him. The son of a Suquamish leader and a Duwamish woman, he was usually regarded as Duwamish. The date of his birth is not known for certain but is considered to be between 1786 and 1790.

As a young man, Seattle was a warrior who was widely known for his daring. However, he became convinced that peace was more desirable than war, largely due to the influence of the Christian missionaries who came into the Northwest in the 1830s. Seattle converted to Christianity and took the name of Noah, who was his favorite Biblical character. Many of his tribesmen also converted.

Due to the California Gold Rush, many whites came to settle in the area of Puget Sound, where they were warmly received by the Indians. In his old age, Chief Seattle asked for and received a small tribute from the citizens of the town named after him. When he died he was buried in the Suquamish Indian cemetery near Seattle. He is best known for his famous poem of lament that was given in reply to the Great White Chief in Washington, D.C. in 1854 on the occasion of an offer of an Indian reservation in exchange for large areas of Indian land.

Secunda, Brant Brant Secunda is an accomplished *shaman* who served an apprenticeship with Don José Matsuwa at the Huichol shaman of Mexico. He is the ceremonial leader and director of the Dance of the Deer Foundation Center for Shamanic Studies. Secunda teaches the Huichol tradition all over the world.

Sedna See *Eskimo, Whales*.

Seminole See *Osceola*.

Seneca See *Iroquis*.

Sequoyah Sequoyah was the founder of the *Cherokee syllabary*. His mother was a Cherokee of mixed blood and his father was white. He was born in Tennessee about 1760 and grew up in the wilderness as a Cherokee. Along with most of his people, he could not read or write English, but when he was lamed in a hunting accident, he turned his attention to trying to educate himself. In a white mission, he taught himself to read and write, and this enabled him to eventually work out the Cherokee alphabet. In doing so, he opened a whole new world of knowledge to his people, who acquired a printing press and published parts of the Holy Bible and a newspaper called *Phoenix*.

Serpent Based on *Sun Bear*'s Earth Astrology, the serpent is the totem of those born between 24 October and 21 November. This old, mysterious, maligned and misunderstood member of the Vertebrata family is a limbless reptile with expandable jaws, slender, inwardly-sloping teeth set toward the back of the mouth, and no ear openings or movable eyelids. The back of the snake contains many vertebrae, sometimes up to 300. The ribs are loosely attached to allow the snake to loop itself around, which is part of the way in which it moves. It also has a large row of belly scales, called 'scutes', each overlapping the one behind it, with the free edge pointing backward. By reaching forward with each scute while pressing backward, the snake is able to glide.

The snake's forked tongue is a very delicate instrument, able to give its owner the senses of both taste and smell. What the tongue picks up is analyzed by a special organ on the roof of the mouth. Snakes have an excellent sense of smell and, generally, of sight. They are carnivorous, mainly eating small animals such as rats and frogs. They will also eat insects, for example flies and mosquitoes. They are very adaptable to their environment and exquisitely sensitive to touch and vibration, partly because they are cold-blooded and are dependent on their environment for warmth. Snakes have no voice, but some can hiss. They are both live-bearing and egg-laying. Most young snakes are born in the warm summer months.

The serpent was respected in most Indian cultures. The feathered serpent was the foremost symbol of the ancient Mayan and Aztec empires, representing the transforming powers that their religions gave them (see also *Quetzalcoatl*), while the *Hopi* feel that the snake is a messenger from other realms and has the capacity to bring life-giving rains. The *Chippewa* people believe that the snake represents patience, since he is so slow to anger, and the Snake Clan was one of their *medicine clans*. Most other *tribes* also attribute special powers to the snake, and many have Snake Clans that perform special functions.

Serpent Mound The Great Serpent Mound, located in Locust Grove, Ohio, is an astounding earthwork that depicts an uncoiled snake with a large oval egg in its mouth. The effigy is attributed to the Adena Indians who lived in close proximity to the Hopewell. Artefacts of both *tribes* have been found in other mounds nearby (see also *Mound Builders*). It is believed that the Serpent Mound could be 3,000 years old. It is built completely from earth and measures 1,348 feet in length, 20 feet in width, and is between four and five feet in height. The serpent's open mouth is 17 feet across. The Great Serpent Mound was not a burial mound, but with the serpent being a universal symbol of wisdom and creativity, it is thought that it was a *sacred site* to its builders, and there is some speculation that it had some special connection to the stars.

Shalako Shalakos are *kachina*s of the *pueblo* people, primarily the *Hopi* and the *Zuni*. The Zuni Shalako ceremony takes place in the winter. It is held over a 49-day period and is known as the House Blessing Ceremony. The ceremony is a re-enactment of the Zuni's *emergence* and migration history. In it prayers are made for propagation and tribal well-being. It is believed to be the time when the dead return so that they can be honored and fed. Ten months are needed to prepare for this ceremony. Special houses must be built or old ones renovated, for eight houses are needed for the Shalakos and one for Sayatasha, the Rain Power of the North, and the Council of Powers. This is called the Long Horn House. Another house is needed for the Mudheads (see *Hopi, Kachina*). The Shalakos are the 'couriers' of the rainmakers.

Shaman A shaman is a *medicine* person, male or female, in an Indian tribe. Shamans possess supernatural powers that they acquire during a vision or ceremonial (see also *Animal Lodge*). Shamanic knowledge includes the use of herbs for *healing*, the power of animals, plants, and stones, celestial knowledge and spirit communication.

Shasta The Shastas were composed of a group of *tribes* in northern California near the Klamath River and in the Mount Shasta Valley. They lived in villages in half-sunken wooden houses, and were fishermen, mainly of salmon, which they dried and smoked. They also made nets, spears and traps for fishing and ate acorns, roots and seeds and hunted for small game with the *bow*. Due to the influx of gold miners and prospectors, the Shasta Indians are now practically extinct. Mount Shasta is a sacred mountain to many tribes in the area.

Shawnodese Based on *Sun Bear*'s Earth Astrology, Shawnodese is the Spirit Keeper of the South, the power of growth and trust. Shawnodese's season is the summer, when all of the Earth's children grow rapidly and come to maturity, trusting in the wisdom of the Earth that allows them to grow and mature properly. Shawnodese's time of day is midday, when the warmth of the sun has helped the buds of dawn to open to the blossoms of the day. In human terms, his time is the time of adulthood, when both the internal and external seeds of youth begin to grow and blossom and the particular purposes of life begin to become clear.

Shields Shields were made from heavy rawhide and were used by the Indians for protection in battle and from all sources of harm. The sight of a shield could strike terror in the hearts of the enemy, making it a prized possession. While not in use, shields would be protected by a cover of soft *buckskin* and hung in a place of honor inside the dwelling. They were painted with sacred symbols, animals and birds.

Shivona See *Zuni*.

Shoshone The Shoshone Indians are of the Uto-Azectan linguistic family, related to the *Comanches*, *Kiowas*, Paiutes and *Hopi*. At one time they held vast amounts of land, living in the Great Basin and clawing a living out of the desert between the Wasatch Mountains and the Sierra Nevada. Then the *Sioux* and other *tribes* came into the Great Basin and the Shoshones became horsemen, hunters and migrants. Some went north and east into Wyoming country and became known as the Northern and Eastern Shoshones, while those who remained in the Great Basin were called the Western Shoshones. The Plains people and the *Utes* raided them and sold them into slavery in Spanish markets in what is now New Mexico.

In 1863 they were given 44.6 million acres by the United States government in what is now Montana, Colorado, Idaho, Utah and Wyoming, and today the Shoshones own but a small portion of the land that was once theirs. Two thousand of them share 1.9 million acres with the Arapahoes in Wyoming on the Wind River Reservation.

Sioux Called 'Adders' by the *Chippewa*, the Sioux were once the very image of the fighting American Indians. Terms that have been used to describe them include 'audacious', 'bold', and 'arrogant'. As warriors, they were superior to all others. They fought other *tribes* for over 200 years and the whites for 50 years. Physically, the Sioux were tall and lithe with high-bridged noses and broad cheekbones which gave them a noble appearance. When they got *horses* they became masterful horsemen and *buffalo* hunters. They were courageous to the point of absolute folly. Beneath it all, however, the Sioux were, and remain, a deeply religious people with a strict and unwavering code of morality. Their spiritual values were instilled through rituals, one of the most famous of which is the *Sun Dance*.

The Sioux called themselves Dakotas, which means 'Allies'. The bands within what they called the Seven Council Fires were the Tetons, Brules, Hunkpapas, Miniconjous, Oglalas, Two Kettles, Sans Arcs, and Blackfeet. Of them all, the Tetons were known to be the most militant.

Today the Great Plains is the home of the Sioux, but that was not always so. They once were scattered over a wide range of territory from Florida to Virginia and North and South Carolina. When their great migrations began to occur around 1500 AD, some pushed west to the Pacific, while others moved to what is now the states of Kentucky, Ohio, Minnesota, Wisconsin and northeastern Iowa. By the early 1700s they had crossed the Missouri River. In the Dakotas they consolidated their bands and became virtually undefeatable. By 1800 they controlled the west bank of the Mississippi River and dominated the area between the Platte River and Canada and from Minnesota to Yellowstone. Eventually they pushed to the Powder River country of Montana.

The whites came to Sioux territory in about 1840. The Sioux attacked their settlements, killing many and taking others hostage. This brought out the United States Cavalry and the ensuing battles were terrible. Many died on both sides, but soon the end of the Sioux domination was in sight. By the time the war was over, some of the Indians were still free, but others were rounded up and put on reservations. At one time, the state of Minnesota placed a $25 bounty on Sioux scalps, resulting in many deaths, and causing the relations between the whites and the Indians to worsen still further.

Today most of the Sioux live on reservations in the Dakotas—there are nine Sioux reservations in South Dakota and two in North Dakota. They continue to speak and write the Dakota language. The Osage, Iowa, Missouri, Quapaw, Ponda, Oto, Kaw and Omaha Sioux still live in Wisconsin and Nebraska, while the Catawbas are in South Carolina and the Biloxi live on the Gulf Coast.

Sipapu Sipapu is the *Hopi* people's place of *emergence* from the Underworld. They say it is a physical place, a yellow pool located at the confluence of the Colorado and the Little Colorado rivers in the Grand Canyon, 60 miles east of Oraibi. It is held to be the exact site of their entrance into the Fourth World, i.e. the present world. A ritual associated with this *sacred site*, sometimes referred to as the 'place of blue salt', concerns the gathering of salt used in *ceremonies*. The Hopi consider the Colorado River to be a symbol of the water that is so important to their arid environment, and the Grand Canyon to be a symbol of the mountainous wall that extends throughout the Fourth World.

Sipapuni Sipapuni, which means 'hole', is truly a sacred opening for spiritual regeneration, the *Hopi* basic concept of *emergence*. The opening in the *kiva*, subterranean temple of the Hopi, symbolizes *Sipapu*, the entrance into the Fourth World, our present world, while the opening or soft spot in a human's head corresponds to sipapuni. The Hopi say that their ancestors were able to freely communicate with the Creator through this opening, but that today it is almost always closed, due to mankind's departure from right living.

Sitting Bull Known as Tatanka Yotanka by his people, Sitting Bull was a Hunkpapa *medicine man* who was killed in 1891. Along with Little Crow, another warrior, he led the *Sioux* uprising of 1864 in Minnesota. He had asked government agents for *food* because his people were starving, and been told to eat grass! It was this treatment that drove the Sioux on the warpath. Sitting Bull was also a *Ghost Dancer*.

Sky Beings Sky Beings are those spirits who inhabit the Sky Country, that is, the heavens. They include (depending upon the legends and beliefs of the tribe concerned): the *sun*, *moon* and stars, Spider Man, Morning Star, Evening Star and the planets.

Slow Turtle Slow Turtle, known to some as John Peters, is a *medicine man* for the Wampanoag Nation, and Director of Indian Affairs for the State of Massachusetts. He travels extensively, teaching the tradition of his people.

Smith, Captain John See *Powhatan*.

Smohala Smohala was the teacher of *Wovoka*, the Paiute who was responsible for bringing the *Ghost Dance* to the Indians.

Smudging Smudging is a ceremony that is used by many Indian *tribes*. *Sun Bear* has introduced it to his students worldwide. It is a process of using smoke to clear away negative energies and attract positive energies to an individual or group.

For smudging, you need a big shell, a piece of pottery or a stone bowl. In this, you should mix *sage* and sweetgrass. If these herbs cannot be found, a high grade of *tobacco* may be used, for tobacco, like sage, draws negativity out of things. The sweetgrass brings in positive energy. Other plants, cedar and juniper for example, may also be used because of their special *healing* powers.

First the mixture should be lit and allowed to smolder. Then the smoke should be drawn toward the heart and over the head to receive its blessings. It is good to use a feather or a fan to keep the mixture smoking well. After you have smudged yourself, you should offer the smoke to the *four directions*, then you may smudge any other people or objects you wish. People should form a *circle* to be smudged, and the smudge should be passed around in a sunwise direction.

Healers have found that smudging is very helpful when it is used to cleanse their offices before other patients arrive. Smudging is also an essential first step before performing a ceremony of any kind.

Snake Dance The Snake Dance is a 16-day rite that is today practiced only by the *Hopi* but was once performed by all the *pueblo*s along the Rio Grande.

The *dance* evolved from a legend in which a youth who sought the source of the Colorado River encountered *Spider Woman*, who helped him find the Great Snake who rules all the waters of the world from his *kiva*. The youth was adopted by the Snake People and married a young girl who changed into a snake. He was given power by Spider Woman and made the Antelope Chief, a chief who instructs his people in the wisdom and *ceremonies* of the Snake People.

Eight days before the public part of the Snake Dance, the snakes, both poisonous and non-poisonous, are gathered during a four-day hunt. They must include one from each of the four cardinal directions. During the hunt, all snakes seen are blessed and taken. Altars and *sandpaintings* are made in the kivas of the Snake and Antelope Societies and secret rites are held each day, with the snakes being carried to the Snake Kiva where they are washed and blessed again. At sunrise on the eighth day, the Snake Priests take the snakes into their mouth and hands. Each priest has a partner who serves as a 'distractor' to the snakes by 'tickling' them with an *eagle*-feather snake whip. Then the dance takes place, and when it is over, the men gather round a *circle* made of cornmeal. The snakes are then thrown into the circle and cornmeal is sprinkled on them before they make their escape.

The Snake Dance is a rain dance and the snakes serve as messengers to take the Hopi prayers to the Rain Spirits.

Snow Goose Snow geese were so named because people did not know where they went when they migrated in the spring, but it was found that they traveled to their northern nesting grounds just as soon as the snow and ice began to melt and they returned when the snow began to fall in the autumn.

Some species of snow goose travel 5,000 miles each year from their nesting grounds in the Canadian subarctic to the Gulf of Mexico and then back again. In their migration they fly a loose V pattern, usually with an adult female as the lead goose. Each goose helps to break the air for those following. They fly slightly to one side of the goose ahead so that they can have unobstructed vision. Snow geese are very gregarious birds. When they are migrating, it is common to see 20–30,000 birds stopping to eat at the same site. At their nesting site they show respect by allowing the experienced nesters to have first choice, and keep their nests about 20 feet apart. Snow geese are cautious parents. After the eggs hatch, the parents moult their primary feathers, which means that they are flightless for the first three to four weeks of their offspring's life. The young birds can fly at about the age of six weeks.

The snow goose is highly respected by the *Chippewa* Indians and is the totem of the Earth Renewal Moon (see *moon*) and of people born between 22 December and 19 January, according to *Sun Bear*'s Earth Astrology.

Sotuknang See *Hopi*, *Taiowa*.

South Star The Skidi *Pawnee* believed that the South Star, sometimes called the Midway Star or the Death Star, presided over the spirits of the dead. Although it is not known for certain, it is thought that the South Star was the *sun* Canopus. It was considered to be the source of tornadoes and its appearance signalled the approach of the winter half of the year.

Soyal Soyal is a great ceremonial of the *Hopi*. Held at the *winter solstice*, the beginning of the new year, during the time between the first appearance of the first-quarter *moon* and the last appearance of the last-quarter moon, Soyal represents the second phase of Creation which brought the dawn of life. The ceremony sets the unfolding life patterns for the coming year. There are no public *dances* during this ceremony and the secret *kiva* rituals are followed by silence, *fasting* and a long period of contemplation.

Spider Man See *Star Country*.

Spider Rock Located on *Canyon de Chelly* on the *Navajo* Reservation in northeastern Arizona, Spider Rock juts more than 800 feet from the desert floor. To geologists, it represents 230 million years of the Earth's history, but to the Navajo Indians, it is much more.

According to the Navajo creation myth, their most important deity, *Spider Woman*, the Creator, along with Monster Slayer and Born of Water, the twin sons of *Changing Woman*, fulfilled the difficult tasks that allowed them to visit their father, the *sun*, to learn from him how to rid the land of monsters who were destroying the people of the Fourth World, that is, our own world. When the monsters were killed, Spider Woman came to live on Earth atop the tallest of the two needles of Spider Rock. Talking God lives on the smaller needle and informs her of the Earth children who misbehave, resulting in her spinning a web and going down and snatching the bad children and, after carrying them back to her home, eating them up. It is the sun-bleached bones of bad kids that tint the white top of Spider Woman's home, in sharp contrast to the otherwise red color of the rock.

Spider Woman Spider Woman, called Kokyangwuti by the *Hopi*, was created out of the First World to remain on the Earth and be the helper for Sotuknang, the First Power. Spider Woman, in turn, took some earth, mixed it with saliva and created two beings whom she covered with a cape made from a white substance which was the creative wisdom itself. Over this, she sang the Creation Song. The two beings, twins named Poquanghoya and Palongawhoya, were given the tasks of helping keep the world in order after life was put upon it and to make the Earth an instrument of sound for the purposes of carrying messages and resounding praise to the Creator. Spider Woman is also known to other *pueblo* people as the Creator. (See also *Spider Rock*.)

Spokane See *Tribes*.

Spotted Eagle, Grace Grace Spotted Eagle was the wife of *Wallace Black Elk*, elder teacher/storyteller and grandson to *Black Elk*, the famed Ogalala holy man. During her life, Grandmother Grace taught about the *Sioux* women's role in family and ceremonial life and about the traditional Sioux way.

Star Bundles Star Bundles were unique to the Skidi band of the *Pawnee* Indians of Nebraska. There were bundles for each village and household. They contained various sacred objects and each represented some element of Pawnee spirituality. The Star Bundles included the Rains-Enfolded Bundle which was opened at the time of the first thunder of spring, causing the clouds to open and rain to fall; the Ant Bundle, the bundle of the Asking-for-Meat Band; the Racoon Bundle of the Little-Earth-Lodge Band; Skull Bundle, which was believed to hold the bones of the first human on Earth; and the North Star Bundle, which was associated with the Chief Ceremony that was conducted for the welfare of the people. (The chiefs were believed to be the mediators between the people and deities.)

The most important bundles were those which represented the powers of the four quarters of the world. These were known as the White Star Bundle, the Yellow Star Bundle, the Red Star Bundle, and the Black Star Bundle. (See also *Quarter Stars*.)

The Morning Star and Evening Star Bundles were common to all villages. The Evening Star Bundle was the supreme bundle and held within it the power of all Creation. Its contents were said to be two ears of *corn*, symbolizing *food*, two owlskins, for the watchfulness of the chiefs, a hawkskin, for the ferocity of the warriors, a piece of flint, for *fire*, and sweetgrass, for incense. The bundle was wrapped in a yellow *buffalo* calf hide and was painted with the colors of the *four directions*. The Evening Star Bundle was kept in an *earth lodge* called the Old Lady Lucky Leader's lodge and was opened in the spring to signal the beginning of the Creation Ceremony.

Star Country Star Country is a land in the sky that is home to the Star People. It holds the lodge of Spider Man, who weaves the ladders by which the Star People travel between the sky and the Earth, and the *tipis* of the *sun* and *moon*. Star Country is much like the Earth, with hills and grassy plains, tipis and campfires.

A *Sioux* legends tells of a young woman named Feather Woman who loved the morning star. One day, while on a trip to gather wood, she ran into a young man who wore a robe of white *buckskin* that was decorated with porcupine quills. He wore *eagle feathers* in his hair and carried a juniper bush that was full of cobwebs. Frightened, Feather Woman started to run but was stopped by the youth, who identified himself as Morning Star. He invited her to return to Star Country with him. Her adventure was a marvelous one! She met Spider Man and the sun and moon. She also learned that the cranes were the enemies of the Star People and that they loved to tear down the ladders made by Spider Man so that the stars would fall to Earth and die. The Indians believe that puff-balls are the remains of dead stars. But, finally becoming homesick, Feather Woman wanted to return to her people and the Earth. When she did, however, she was not happy for she missed her husband and her home in Star Country. Every night, with their son, Star Boy, in her arms, Feather Woman climbed to the top of the western hills and watched for Morning Star. Finally, she got up the courage to speak to him and beg him to take her back. But it was not to be. Morning Star replied that it was too late and that she could never return. This made Feather Woman very unhappy and lonely, and she died of a broken heart.

Storytellers The storytellers are the bards of the Indian *tribes*. It is with them that the legends and myths of the people reside. Storytellers share their stories during certain *ceremonies* and for entertainment. They are also teachers of the tradition of their particular tribes. The storytellers of the *pueblos* in the southwest are depicted in art with large numbers of children perched on their arms, shoulders, and lap during the telling of tales.

Sturgeon Based on *Sun Bear*'s Earth Astrology, the sturgeon is the totem of those born between 23 July and 22 August. King of fishes, it is an old and primitive fish that has probably existed on the Earth since about the time that the dinosaurs disappeared. Depending on its location and species, it comes in a variety of sizes, but can reach 12 feet in length and 300 pounds in weight. Sturgeons have rows of bony plates on their body, making their skin especially tough. They have a long snout with the mouth on the underside, and four barbels, or sense organs, on the underside of the snout. Their tail lobes are unequal in size, with the upper being the larger. Their skeletons are usually mainly cartilage.
    Sturgeons live in the mud bottoms off coasts, and usually reach sexual maturity at about 20 years of age, The females then spawn in spring or early summer, going upstream or moving to shallow water. They lay two million or more eggs, but probably do not spawn every year.

Sun The sun played an important role in the lives of Indian people throughout the North American continent, and many Indians called it 'Grandfather Sun'.
    The earliest Indian calendars were based on the sun, being *mountains*, rock crevices or man-made objects that marked its rising and setting from a particular place, a method of keeping track of time that has been used worldwide. The Indians of the Southwest are particularly noted for their solar horizon calendars. An example may be seen in a member of the *Hopi* priesthood known as the 'Sunwatcher' who has memorized the important points of sunset against the San Francisco Peaks, sacred mountains located in Flagstaff, Arizona. At the *winter solstice* the sun sets to the south of the peaks, then the sunset slowly shifts northward, up the slopes of the mountains, reaching the highest peak in January before moving down the north slopes. When the sun moves to the north of the peaks, the Indians know that it is time to prepare the fields for planting.
    Shrines were often built to the sun, the most famous of which is the

so-called Sun Temple at Mesa Verde, Colorado. Built by the ancient cliff dwellers, the Sun Temple was most likely used for ceremonial purposes. It is believed by some to be the site of the Hopi legendary temple that was built by their ancestors. The ancestors were struck with a confusion of tongues and had to leave the temple unfinished. After that, they moved to the south and established the present Hopi villages.

The Skidi people believed that the sun was the brother of the Morning Star and father of the people, while *Zuni* Sun Priests are in charge of bringing the new *fire* that opens the ceremonial season each year.

Sun Bear Sun Bear is a *Chippewa medicine man*, and medicine chief of the *Bear Tribe Medicine Society* located east of Spokane, Washington. He is also the publisher of *Wildfire*, a magazine dedicated to being a voice of and for the Native American people and their way of life, and the author of *At Home in the Wilderness*, *Buffalo Hearts* and *The Bear Tribe's Self-Reliance Book*.

Sun Bear was born on the White Earth Reservation in northern Minnesota on 31 August 1929. His father, Louis, was a Chippewa Indian with some French blood, while his mother, Judith, came from German/Norwegian stock. His grandmother worked with herbs which she used for *healing*, and his grandfather was an engagée for the Hudson's Bay Company. Sun Bear has 10 brothers and sisters in all.

Sun Bear has taught Native American philosophy at the University of California, Davis, and has lectured on the traditional Native way to groups in many countries, including the United States, Canada, Britain, Germany, New Zealand, Australia, Mexico and Egypt. The full story of his life has been told in *Path of Power* by *Wabun Wind* and Barry Weinstock.

Sun Dance Known as Wiwanyag Wachipi, the Sun Dance is one of the greatest of the sacred rites of the *Sioux*. It was first held long after the people had received the pipe from *White Buffalo Woman*. The Sun Dance is held each year during the Moon of Fattening in June or during the Moon of Cherries Blackening in July; in either case, when the *moon* is full. To the Sioux, the full moon represents the eternal light of the *Great Spirit* upon the Earth.

Legend has it that the Sun Dance came to the people when they were camped in a *circle* having council. One of the men, named Kablaya, dropped his robe to his waist and started dancing alone, his hand raised towards the heavens. Thinking that he was crazy, the old men sent someone to find out what was wrong. However, the man that was sent suddenly dropped his own robe to his waist and starting

dancing with Kablaya. When the others went over to see what was
going on, Kablaya told them that the people were not living right and
were lax in their smoking of the sacred pipe and other *ceremonies*. He
said that he had just been shown in a vision a new way of praying.
The men were pleased and asked Kablaya to tell them what to do. He
said that they were to perform a sacred Sun Dance, and that they
must wait for four days before doing the *dance*, which would be an
offering of their bodies and souls to the Great Spirit, *Wankan-Tanka*.
He then instructed the old and holy men of the tribe to build a large
tipi, into which they should put *sage*. They should also have ready a
pipe, some Ree twist *tobacco*, the bark of the red willow, sweetgrass,
a bone knife, a tanned *buffalo* calf hide, some rabbit skins, some *eagle*
plumes, red earth paint, a flint axe, buffalo tallow, rawhide, blue
paint, a buffalo skull, a rawhide bag, some eagle tail *feathers* and
whistles made from the wing bones of the Spotted Eagle.

When the people had gotten these things together, Kablaya asked
those that could sing to come so that he could teach them the sacred
songs. They were to bring with them a *drum* and drumsticks made
from buffalo hide with the hair side out. Kablaya told the people that
in the sacred dance there was to be a cottonwood tree at the center
of a circle to represent the way of the people, with an eagle plume tied
to it. He then taught the people four songs and showed how the eagle
whistles were to be used, as well as all the other sacred objects. He
also said that a five-pointed star should be cut from rawhide to
symbolize Morning Star, who stands between darkness and light and
represents knowledge. They were also to make a round rawhide circle
and to paint it red with its center blue, to represent the sun and the
Great Spirit. Another round circle should be cut and painted red for
the Earth and the Sacred Mother and yet another which would be
painted blue for the heavens. Finally, they should cut a buffalo figure
out of rawhide, to represent the people and the universe who must
always be treated with respect. Every man was to wear one of these
sacred symbols and know of their meaning. The people then went
into a tipi to receive further instructions and to purify all the sacred
objects.

The warriors painted and dressed themselves and entered the
sacred lodge which was built in a circle out of 28 poles in honor of
the lunar cycle, each day of which is sacred in some way to the Sioux
people. The buffalo has 28 ribs and in their war bonnets the Sioux
used 28 eagle feathers. The dancers danced toward the west first,
then to the center, then to the north and to the center again, to the
east, to the center, and finally to the south and then back to the
center, their path making the shape of a cross. Kablaya entered into
the lodge carrying the sacred pipe. All the buffalo robes to be used

in the dance were put on top of the lodge to be purified. Five hot rocks representing five of the six directions were brought in and placed on an altar; a sixth one placed on the sacred path.

On the morning of the third day, the dancers were pierced through the muscles of their backs and skewers of bone were inserted. A number of buffalo skins were then tied to the skewers with thongs. The dancers, crying out, dragged the heavy skins until the flesh gave way.

Then, around noon on the fourth day, the dancers ran around the center pole of the lodge until they fainted from exhaustion. A priest then waved his buffalo-tail fan over them until they revived. When the last of them had been revived, they each told of their visions. This is how the Sun Dance is still performed today.

During the Sun Dance, each dancer wears a wreath of sage on his head, which represents the things of heavens, the stars and planets. Bodies are painted red from the waist up, with a black circle around the face with a black line drawn from the forehead to a point between the eyes and on each side of the cheek and on the chin, representing the *four directions*. Black stripes are painted around the wrists, elbows, upper arms and ankles. Black is the color of ignorance and the stripes are the bonds that tie humans to the Earth.

The dancers also purify themselves with the smoke from sweetgrass. After the dance, the men go back to the sacred tipi where a feast is held while all the people rejoice.

The Indians believe that the Sun Dance will give them much strength and will give life to their nation. It has been adopted by many *tribes* and is still widely practiced today. It is called the New-Life Lodge by the *Cheyenne*, and the Mystery Dance by the *Ponca*. The Okapi Ceremony of the Mandans was also very similar. To all Native people, the Sun Dance is a celebration of the renewal of life, 'to make the grass grow and the buffalo and the people increase and thrive.' It is also a time for young men to find wives and for old people to renew friendships.

Sun Shrines Many Indian *tribes* had special places where they went to honor 'Grandfather Sun' and/or to observe the *sun*. The *Chumash* people marked these places with feathered poles. Other *sacred sites* such as the Bighorn *Medicine Wheel* and *Chaco Canyon* were known to have been oriented to sunrise on the summer solstice.

Sunstick The sunstick was used by the *Chumash* Indians of California, in ancient times, to honor the *sun*. The stick was stood upright in the ground. The High Chief portrayed the image of the sun and 12 priests were the solar rays.

Sweat Lodge See *Inipi*.

Swiftdeer, Harley Harley Swiftdeer is a *Cherokee/Metis medicine man*, founder of the Deer Tribe, and teacher of the *Sun Dance* way and of White Crystal Medicine. Swiftdeer resides in California but teaches throughout the world.

Syllabary The syllabary is the *Cherokee* alphabet. It was the first written system of communication amongst the Indian people and had a profound influence upon their lives (see also *Sequoyah*).

T

Totem Pole

Tablets When the *Hopi* emerged into the Fourth World, the present world, they were told how to make their migrations by Masaw, the Earth's guardian spirit (see also *Emergence*). Masaw outlined the migrations, how the people could recognize where they were to settle permanently and the way they were to live in symbols on four sacred stone tablets. The first of the tablets was entrusted to the Fire Clan, the other three to the Bear Clan. The tablets confirmed the rights of the Hopi to their land.

These sacred tablets are said to still be in the possession of the Hopi, though some have disappeared or been lost. The small Fire Clan tablet is said to have appeared in Phoenix in 1942, at the American entry into the Second World War, when several Hopi men were being tried for refusing to be drafted into military service. It is now reported to be in the possession of the Fire Clan leader in Hotevilla on Third Mesa.

Tablita See *Corn Dance*.

Taiowa Taiowa is the *Hopi* Indians' name for the Creator. In the beginning, all life, time, shape and space was in his mind. When Taiowa conceived the finite, he created Sotuknang, the First Power, to make it manifest. As he was instructed, Sotuknang gathered what was to be made manifest from endless space, moulded it into forms and set them into nine universal kingdoms. One of the kingdoms was for Taiowa, another for himself, and the other seven were for life to come.

Talking God See *Spider Rock*.

Talking Stick The talking stick was used as a tool for keeping order among some Indian *tribes*. During council, the person holding the stick was allowed to speak without interruption. When he or she had finished, it was passed to the next person who wished to speak.

Tanakwatawa See *Tecumseh*.

Taos The Taos *pueblo* is one of the eastern settlements of the Rio Grande. According to tradition, the Taos people followed a bird to the foot of the sacred pueblo peak where they founded villages. It is widely believed by archeologists that the Taos people came from Mexico and were offshoots of the Aztec stock.

Tapa Wanka Yap This was a ball game played at one time by the *Sioux*, consisting of four teams and four goals which were set up in each of the *four directions*. The rules of the game and its hidden meaning were received by a Lakota called Moves Walking in a vision.

Today recognized by few as sacred, Tapa Wanka Yap was an important rite representing the course of a person's life. This should be spent in getting the ball, which represents the *Great Spirit*, *Wankan-Tanka*. The Sioux say this is a difficult task, for ignorance can keep one from reaching this goal. Only a few succeed. However, in the early days, everyone was able to have the ball, meaning that everyone had the power of Wankan-Tanka easily within reach. This was because of the values of that time. Now humans have strayed from those values, and the achievement of 'getting the ball' is far more difficult.

Tatanka Yotanka See *Sitting Bull*.

Tawakiiks See *Animal Lodge*.

Tecumseh Tecumseh was born to the *Shawnee* tribe in what is now Ohio in 1768. His name meant Shooting Star. He witnessed the encroachment and westward movement of the Americans after the Revolutionary War, and tried to unite all the *tribes* against the white man's expansion. He went from tribe to tribe on this mission, from Creeks in the south and the *Sioux* and the *Chippewa* in Minnesota, clear to the Canadian border.

For a time, Tecumseh and his brother worked together. His brother was called Tanakwatawa, the Open Door. He was referred to by the whites as 'The Prophet', and when they established an Indian town at Tippecanoe River in Indiana, it was called Prophet Town.

Tecumseh was once in love with a beautiful white girl, and she wanted to marry him, but she told him he must give up his Indian ways and this he could not do.

In 1811, while Tecumseh was south on a trip recruiting other tribes to his cause, William Henry Harrison, the Governor of Indian Territory, attacked Prophet Town. The Indians fought back, but being in small numbers, they were forced to abandon their town. Tecumseh was very angry with his brother for allowing the Indians to be drawn into battle before the time he had set. Now there was raiding by other tribes along the frontier, but no united effort. The following year, 1812, Tecumseh joined the British in his fight against the raiding parties of other Indians, bringing with him an army of between one and three thousand warriors.

In the War of 1812, it was Tecumseh's warriors who were the deciding factor in the capture of Detroit. All during that war, Tecumseh showed himself an able general and a brave warrior. One of the British commanders allowed the Indians who were fighting with them to kill and torture prisoners. When one of Tecumseh's men told him of this, he stormed over to the camp, knocked down the Indians who had killed and tortured, and called them cowards for their deeds of destroying defenseless men. He also told the British commander that he was unfit to command.

When General Harrison marched against the British with a force of 3,500 troops while the British had only 700 men and Tecumseh's 1,000 Indians, General Proctor began to retreat, although Tecumseh wanted him to stand and fight. With the first attack, the British general fled and the British troops surrendered. However, Tecumseh ordered his people to fight on and, even though wounded many times, he himself continued to fight. But when darkness came over the battlefield, a bullet struck and killed him. His men would not leave his body to be found and it was taken away and buried. Thus ended the life of a great Shawnee.

Teepee See *Tipi*.

Teton See *Sioux*.

Tewa The Tewa live in the northern Rio Grande *pueblos* of *Taos* and Picuris, and the more southern villages of Sandia and *Isleta*. In the early days, they grew *corn*, squash, *beans* and melons. They wore clothes made of cotton and long robes made of *feathers*. Around the end of the sixteenth century the Tewa were invaded by the Spaniards, who killed most of the men and took the women and children into slavery. The Tewas also lived with the *Hopi* people in Arizona and continue to do so today.

Thought Woman Thought Woman is the deity who created all things by thinking them into existence. She is revered by the Indians of the Rio Grande *pueblos*, and thought to be the same figure as Spider Grandmother, or *Spider Woman*, who possesses the same attributes.

Thunder Beings According to the Indians of ancient times, Thunder Beings are the 'Voice of the Sky Father'. They bring rain to make life grow on the Earth and send warnings of danger to the people.

Sun Bear works with the Thunder Beings as part of his *medicine*. They give him much information as to the state of world affairs and prophecies that concern the future of mankind and the planet. Sun Bear also calls upon the Thunder Beings in his prayers to bring rain in drought-stricken areas.

Thunder Ritual The Thunder Ritual was performed in the spring by the Skidi band of the *Pawnee* Indians for the purpose of renewal of the flow of life. Thunder and lightning put life into lifeless forms in the spring, the season of creation. The Thunder Ritual was based on the passing of the first spring thunderstorm which vitalized the Earth from west to east. *Tirawahat*, the *Great Spirit*, acting through The Wonderful Being, sent storms to help crops to grow and to replenish the rivers and streams. The Wonderful Being was the ultimate Creator of the Pawnee, the Great Mystery or Great Unknown who created Tirawahat.

At the beginning of the Thunder Ritual, the Evening Star Bundle was opened by its priest, and dancers flitted about to mimic the flickering of the Evening Star.

Thunderbird The Thunderbird, sometimes called the Fire Bird or the phoenix, is a mythological bird that is sacred to many Native peoples. Its work is to water the Earth so that vegetation will grow. Lightning is believed to flash from its beak and the beating of its wings represents thunder. Sometimes the magical bird was represented as having an extra head protruding from its abdomen. The Thunderbird was often accompanied by lesser bird spirits in the form of *eagles* or falcons. Its symbol is often painted on sacred objects, *tipis*, *drums*, and clothing.

Tipi The tipi is an Indian dwelling, used primarily by the Plains people. Native Americans believed that living inside a *circle* helped them to experience the sacred cycle of life. The Plains peoples' tipis were made of heavy *buffalo* hides and had 'liners' in them. The canvas ones used today are serviceable in warm climates, but they are not recommended for cold areas.

Lodge pole pines are used for the frame of the tipi. The trees are first stripped of their branches and bark and then placed in a circle with the tops falling together. Hides are then stretched over the poles with a flap left for the door. *Fires* can be built inside the tipi for the smoke can easily escape through the opening created by the poles leaning together at the top. Some tribes would paint their tipis various colors, and add designs of animals, birds and sacred symbols.

Tirawahat Tirawahat was the name given to the Creator, the Great Cause of All, by the Skidi *Pawnee* Indians of Nebraska. Sometimes called 'The Expanse of the Heavens' and 'Beyond All Others', Tirawahat directed everything. There were four direct paths leading from his house in the sky in the four semi-cardinal directions: northeast, northwest, southeast and southwest. The Pawnee would make offerings from these positions so that Tirawahat's power could be received by the people.

Tiwa See *Tewa*.

Tobacco Indians have used tobacco for pleasure and sacred rites since anyone can remember. Sir Walter Ralegh learned of the use of tobacco from the Indians. When he first lit tobacco in a London pub, the bartender poured water over him, thinking he was on *fire*! Tobacco is sometimes used as a sacred offering to the Earth or to spirit beings (see also *Prayer Ties*).

Tomahawk The tomahawk was a weapon used by Indians in battle and in the hunt. It also served as a cutting tool that came in handy during construction projects. The earliest tomahawks were made of a sharp stone that was tied with rawhide strips to a wooden handle.

Tom-Tom See *Drum*.

Totem Pole The totem pole is a column of wood, usually cedar, that has been carved with figures that have symbolic meaning. They are used only by the northwestern *tribes*, including the Alaskan tribes. Various poles show animals, fish, birds and creatures from tales and legends. For example, the mountain goat is a symbol of nobility, the *moon* represents height or status, the grizzly *bear* embodies strength and ferocity, and the killer whale is known as the ruler of the seas and the Underworld. A symbol of a given family is often carved into the pole, so it is not unlike the Coats of Arms of the British culture. The poles are brightly painted and can be very beautiful.

Trail of Tears Brought about by the Indian Removal Act of 1830, the Trail of Tears was the name given to the deadly march of the *Cherokees* to the Indian Territory west of the Mississippi River in Oklahoma. The trek was over 800 miles long and the Indians were forced to make it on foot. During the six months that it took to reach the Indian Territory, 1,000 of the 4,000 Cherokees died. Today, a drama called the 'Trail of Tears' is performed by the Western Cherokees to commemorate the march.

Tree Burials Tree burials were practiced by the Indians along the Mississippi River. When a child died during the time from birth to the end of the first year of life, a hole was carved out in a tree and the body placed inside. The hole was then sealed with bark. The practice ensured that the dead child could experience life through the living tree, and its soul blended with the tree. This ritual was done in the earliest days of Indian history, and when, in later times, the trees were cut, they revealed the bones, as well as *beads* and other items that had been buried with the child.

Tribes A tribe is a group of people who come from a common ancestor and form a community under a common leader. The following are the major Native American tribes:

Pacific Northwest Tribes The Cascade Mountains acted as a barrier through Washington state and Oregon. The territory east of the *mountains* was the plateau country, the west the humid coast. In this land, two Indian cultures evolved. In the eastern uplands were the so-called 'horse Indians' who were greatly influenced by the Plains people. In the west were the 'water Indians', who were fishermen, trappers and timber woodworkers. They also had oceangoing whaleboats and were whalers.

Life was easy for the water Indians. They had plenty of *food*. They mastered the use of traps and nets for fishing and they also speared fish with *bows and arrows* or clubbed them. They were surrounded by evergreen forests made up mostly of red cedars, and used wood for many purposes, the most important of which was for dugouts (a form of boat), shelters and gabled lodges. They used the inside bark for *weaving*. Red cedar lent itself well to making tools and utensils. The Indians would steam and bend the wood and then fashion it into many devices. These people wove excellent *baskets* of dog hair and then decorated them with inlays of bone, copper and shells. In fact, they put elaborate designs on just about everything.

The water Indians had their own aristocracy, a first among Native peoples. Those who were highest had exclusive rights to the best fishing places and were the only ones allowed to build certain craft, as well as being in control of the wealth and social rank. The aristocratic order was: chiefs, who were of royal blood; nobility, the privileged class; common people, who were the workers; and slaves, who were the captives.

The society ritual of the water Indians was the 'Potlatch', a feast and gift-giving ceremonial. The Potlatch provided the opportunity for the people to display their wealth and status and they were lavish and prestigious affairs. Potlatches were given on state occasions such as the initiating of a new chief, and they marked birthdays, adoptions and marriages, and served well to save face after a defeat or failure as well as simply impressing other people.

The horse Indians, who lived east of the Cascades, fished the Snake and Columbia Rivers. They were also *buffalo* hunters who counted their wealth in *horses*. They had little formal organization. Their *ceremonies* were almost perfunctory and only those related to replenishing the food supply were celebrated with any real dedication.

When the white explorers arrived on the Pacific northwest coast, about 50 tribes were living by the bays and rivers, so the Indians got used to seeing ships and white men. By 1750, white traders arrived from the sea and from the great mountains came the Lewis and Clark explorers. This opened a wedge from the east and a surge of adventurers came in. The Indians learned to fur and trap from the whites, but the whites brought disease, suffering, death and war. Some tribes, like the Chinooks, were almost wiped out by smallpox.

Some of the Pacific Northwest tribes are the Colvilles, Spokane and Yakima, who live on reservations in Washington state, and the Umatilla and Warm Springs who live on reservations in Oregon.

Northeastern Tribes The northeastern tribes comprised the *Algonquins* and the *Iroquis*, two large tribal groupings who were engaged in a struggle to the death. Both of the tribes also faced problems brought by the whites—war, disease, liquor and prostitution.

When the British were defeated, the northeastern tribes, who had fought with them, ceded most of their territory to the United States of America. Since that time they lived there only by permission of the whites, and today, there is no federal reservation in the northeast. However, the Indians have left their indelible mark in the form of the names of cities, rivers, townships and so forth. The Algonquins are gone, dispersed across the continent, but there are many Iroquis left.

The *Iroquis League of Six Nations* was the greatest of all Indian confederacies.

Tulugaukuk See *Raven*.

Tumalo Tumalo is the subject of a *Hopi* legend. Once, in a vision, he saw an unmasked *kachina* who knew the secrets of the rain. The being asked Tumalo to keep silent about what he had seen.

Then one day, during a celebration and feast when the kachinas were visiting with the Hopi, a terrible accident occurred and one of the kachinas was killed. This resulted in them feeling great anger for the people that they had opened their hearts to, so they withdrew, coming no more to the villages or walking the land on lightning bolts or on legs of rain. The Hopi began to suffer drought and famine and a tremendous loneliness at the loss of their kachinas. Their hunting skills diminished and they forgot how to grow food ... all except for Tumalo. He had learned a great deal from the kachina and knew of the valuable gifts that the kachinas had brought to his people. But he also realized that the Hopi would now have to fend for themselves.

Seeking to be of some help to his people, Tumalo suggested that they must learn to be like the kachinas, that they must learn to bring the rain and talk to the Earth so that the crops would grow, but the people only laughed at what he said.

Then Tumalo left the village, taking with him some dried *corn* kernels, a bean and the stony seed of a peach that he had found in the ashes of a cooking pit. He took these down to the valley below, planted them and watered them with the last drop of water from his gourd. After blessing the seeds, he set off for the sacred *mountains* in the southwest that he had seen in his dreams. Although the journey was a long and lonely one, Tumalo pushed on. One dawn, he spotted an *eagle* and followed him to the sacred mountains. He knew that he could find the kachinas there.

For three days Tumalo climbed to the summit of the peaks. As he lay sleeping one day, the kachina that he had seen many seasons ago appeared beside him. Tumalo asked him to speak to the other kachinas on behalf of the Hopi. Much to his joy, the kachina returned to say that although the kachinas would not come to the people as they had done before, if the Hopi would make *masks* and impersonate them, they could call for rain and good crops. If this was done sincerely they would have bounty once again.

Tumalo raced back to his village with a glad heart. The masks were made. Returning to the place where he had planted the seeds, Tumalo had a vision in which he received further messages from the kachinas. He went back to the village and told the people to make prayer *feathers* and to sprinkle cornmeal as a path for the kachinas. This is the ceremony of *Soyal*, to be done at the time of the *winter solstice* to bring snow and moisture. Eototo, father of the kachinas, then came and taught all the *dance*s and rituals necessary so that the land and the people would prosper once more, ceremonies that are still performed today.

Tunka See *Yuwipi*.

Turquoise Turquoise is a mineral that is found in many parts of the world, including Arizona, New Mexico, Colorado and Nevada. It was considered by the Indians to be sacred stone that held special potent powers. Some of these include the ability to experience victory over enemies, and the power of bestowing good fortune and helping one find good and steadfast friends. It was also considered to be a strong love charm.

   Turquoise is moderately hard but is easily marred. Its colors range from sky blue to light cerulean blue and from pale to heavy green. There is also a type known as 'spider web' that is laced with black lines throughout the blue stone. The *Navajo* and *Zunis* are known for their beautifully ornate turquoise and silver jewelry, and the Zunis make many of their *fetishes* out of turquoise.

Turtle Island Turtle Island is the name given to the continent of North America by the Indians. The turtle is held in high esteem by many *tribes*. The Sweat Lodge (see *Inipi*) is built in the shape of a turtle in honor of the Earth being borne on the back of a turtle.

Tusayan Pueblo Tusayan pueblo is an ancient *Anasazi* Indian village located about three miles west of Desert View on the *Grand Canyon*'s South Rim. The Anasazi, ancestors of the *Hopi*, lived at the canyon from about 500 to 1200 AD, and the Tusayan village was constructed in about 1185 AD.

Tuscaroras See *Iroquis*.

Tustenuggee See *Osceola*.

Two Kettles See *Sioux*.

U

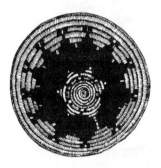

Ute Design Coiled Basket

Umatilla See *Tribes*.

Uncegila Uncegila, also known as Unktehi, was the great water monster of the *Sioux* Indians. She was said to be an evil witch who had been transformed into a snakelike monster when the Earth was very young. She was very long and her body was thicker than the biggest tree trunk in the world and her scales were of glistening mica. She had one curved horn coming out of the top of her head. Along her back ran a crest like flames and her sides were decorated with spots of many colors. The only way she could be killed was if a *medicine* arrow was shot through the seventh spot from her head. Her heart was made of ice-cold *crystal*.

Uncegila was killed by twin boys, one of whom was blind, who got their arrows from Old Ugly Woman, the monster woman of the Sioux. She told the boys to cut out the icy heart and wrap it in thick hide to carry it. They were told that the heart would speak, asking four questions. The boys were warned to refuse to answer four times but after that they must do what the heart wished and they must share the power that the heart gave them.

When the monster was killed and her heart was taken, the boys remembered their instructions. After refusing four questions, they were told that the blind twin should spread some of Uncegila's blood on his eyelid. He did and he could see. The heart was placed in a deep shaft over which was built a special lodge painted with Uncegila's likeness, and it continued to give instructions for special *ceremonies* to the boys, making them very powerful.

Soon, however, the twins tired of their great powers and decided to divest themselves of the burden of the crystal heart. They invited the people to the special lodge and allowed them to look at the cold red crystal heart. While the people were looking, the heart screamed and burst into a ball of *fire*, consuming itself so that only ashes remained. The boys lived happily from then on and felt relieved of the burden of their magical powers. They took good and bad as it came, as most people must do. It is said that now only the bones of Uncegila are left, strewn across the *Badlands* of Nebraska and the Dakotas and that they still possess strong *medicine* powers.

Unktehi See *Uncegila*

Ute The Utes belong to the Uto-Aztecan linguistic family, and are a Shoshonean tribe of western Colorado and eastern Utah. They are closely related, culturally, to the Plains Indians, performing the *Sun Dance* and living in *tipis*. Once they acquired *horses*, they roamed as far south as the *Taos pueblo* in New Mexico and southern Wyoming.

Friendly to the whites, the Utes signed a peace treaty with the U.S. government. Their most well-known chief was Ouray, who had an excellent relationship with the silver miners. The Utes now raise cattle and live on a reservation near Ignacio, Colorado. The northern Utes live on the Ute Mountain Reservation in Colorado and on the Uintah and Ouray Reservations in Fort Duchesne, Utah.

V

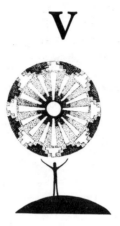

Vision Quest

Victorio Victorio was a brave *Apache* leader who fought with *Mangus Colorado* and *Cochise* in many battles against the U.S. Cavalry in what is now the state of Arizona.

Vision Quest Native Americans did not feel that they were truly complete until they had undertaken a vision quest to communicate with the spirits to gain direction and purpose in their lives. The vision quest, as a rule, lasted up to four days and nights and was preceded by a period of *fasting* and prayer. Usually it was a ritual performed by young men.

Once the decision to go on a vision quest was made, the seeker had to petition the *medicine man* for assistance. He would bring the medicine man *blankets*, a horse or other gifts and, in return, the medicine man would prepare a sacred Sweat ceremony, that is, a rite of purification (see *Inipi*), and make special prayers. The *Sioux* referred to the vision quest as 'crying for a vision'. During the time of the quest, the medicine man would continue to pray. Generally, the seeker would fast during the vision quest, sometimes from both *food* and water. He also took few or no earthly goods with him. A successful vision quest would give the young man answers as to how he might best serve the Creator, his people and the *Earth Mother*.

The following is a *Chippewa* legend told by *Sun Bear*, explaining how the vision quest rite was given to his people.

There was once a man and wife who had no children. This was of deep concern to them because they were getting on in years and they felt strongly that they should have a son. They would take great pride in him and they felt that he would turn out to be an important person in the tribe and a good hunter. Their desires were granted and a son was born to them. The boy did well.

One day there was to be a contest among the young men to see how much game each could kill in one day. The old man bet all of his prized deerskins on his son. But when his son returned from the hunt, he had only three rabbits and three squirrels; all the other boys had more and the old man's son was only second best.

Then another contest came. This time it was a wrestling match. Again, the old man bet many hides and gifts that his son would be the best. But it was not to be so, for his son turned out to be second best again. It was at this point that the old man decided that his son would be a great medicine man, that he would have a powerful vision.

The son fasted and prayed and then he left to go out on the land for four days and four nights to receive his vision. No vision came. The father was not to be daunted so he began to fatten up his son so that he would regain his strength and prepared him for yet another vision quest. The old man never gave a thought to his son having thoughts and feelings in his own heart. He particularly loved to hear his uncle play the flute. But, because he wanted to please his father, he went on the second vision quest. Still no vision came. But the father only began the process of preparing his son for yet another try for a vision. This went on for almost two years.

However, while on what was to be his final quest, the son finally had a vision. He fell into a dream in which he saw many beautiful birds and heard many melodious songs. This was a powerful experience. When the son did not return from his vision quest, his father went to look for him. But he could not find him. Year after year, time after time, the old man searched in vain for his son. On one of his searches, the father noticed a beautiful bird sitting in a tree on the site where the boy had gone for his vision. The bird was singing a beautiful song. The bird followed the old man home and when he lay down to sleep that night, it came to him in a dream and told him that it was his son. 'This is the only way that I can come to you now. I could not be the way you wanted me to be. The last time I prayed a vision came. I became a beautiful bird. To make music is my purpose in life.' The son was known from then on as Medicine Robin.

Another legend about the vision quest that Sun Bear tells concerns

a great warrior who wanted a vision all his life but one had not come.
Every year he went on a vision quest with no results. Finally, during
one of his quests, a spirit came and told him to put aside his weapons
and become a man of peace. He was also told to give gifts to all the
people in the village and to help them in any way he could. The great
warrior did what he was told and no longer went on the warpath.
Young men continued to come to him and beg for leadership but he
refused. He could not just tell them about his vision, he had to live
it! One day, the Peace Chiefs of the tribe came and brought the peace
pipe. They told the warrior that they had been watching him for years
and knew that he had followed his vision faithfully. Now they wanted
him to lead the tribe in the Peace Dance. This made the warrior very
happy and he became a Peace Chief.

W

Wolf Mask of Northwest Design

Wabanakis These Indians were called the 'People of the East' and 'The Children of the Dawn Country'. They were made up of five nations of people: the Passamaquoddy, *Penobscot*, *Micmac*, Malisett and a tribe whose name is now forgotten, who once lived on the Kennebec River. The Wabanakis are of *Algonquin* stock. In the early days, they wore garments made of moose skin and furs. Their dishes were made of wood and bark. They carried pouches made of skins, and made knives and *tomahawks* of stone.

Waboose Based on *Sun Bear*'s Earth Astrology, Waboose is the power of the Spirit Keeper of the North, the power of renewal and purity. The season of Waboose is the winter, when the Earth is lying dormant, seemingly asleep. The daily time of Waboose is the night, when day creatures lie in sleep, the small death, and in human life the time of Waboose is the older years, when hair becomes like snow, when bodies are slower and minds are purified by turning to thoughts of the spirit. Waboose is represented by the white *buffalo*, one of the most sacred of all animals. .

Wabun Based on *Sun Bear*'s Earth Astrology, Wabun is the Spirit Keeper of the East, the power of illumination and wisdom. The season of Wabun is the spring, when the Earth is awakening from the sleep of winter, and the new life which has been preparing itself in the womb of the Earth bursts forth. The daily time of Wabun is dawn, when life awakens from the sleep of night. In human life, the time of Wabun is youth, the time of awakening to things both within and outside, the time when people are capable of illuminating others by the purity of their energy.

Wabun Wind Wabun Wind, also known as Marlise James, joined Sun Bear as his companion and medicine helper in 1972. For the next 16 years she acted as the Bear Tribe's executive director. She is the author or co-author of seven books, director of a communications company, lecturer, teacher for and consultant to the Bear Tribe, a transpersonal practitioner and ceremonial designer. Wabun holds a master's degree from Columbia University. Her latest book is *Woman of the Dawn: A Spiritual Odyssey.*

Wabun's husband, Thomas Wind, was the subchief of the Bear Tribe for several years and coordinator of the Apprentice Screening Program. Thomas is currently a medical student in Pennsylvania. Thomas and Wabun are the parents of an adopted Peruvian daughter, Kyla.

Walpi Walpi is an ancient *Hopi* village located on the western point of First Mesa. The mesa is so narrow in this spot that there is only room for two rows of terraced houses. They step down to the south where *kiva*s are built into the walls of the cliff. The snake kiva is in the plaza about half the length of the village from where Snake Rock stands.

Wampum Wampum *beads* are made from various kinds of shells and were highly prized by the Indians who lived along the Atlantic coast. The beads come in white, pink, and purple from the conch, quahog, and clam shells respectively. Wampum beads were used in many ways, including being strung to make bracelets and necklaces, for decoration on clothing, and as weapons, money and utensils. They were also made into belts and used in the place of signatures to confirm treaties or agreements between *tribes.*

Each bead had its own meaning: white wampum beads symbolized peace and trust, and purple symbolized death and sorrow, while red beads symbolized war and were often sent as an invitation to join a war party. Oftentimes, various colors of beads were combined to convey particular messages or to represent and record *ceremonies.*

Legend has it that the *Iroquis* hero *Hiawatha* made the first wampum beads which he found on a dry lake bed that was covered with shells. He used the beads to unite the tribes in peace.

Wampum Bird An *Iroquis* legend, the Wampum Bird appeared to a young girl who was gathering cranberries in a marsh near her village. Terrified, the girl dropped what she was doing and fled! She described the huge bird as half the height of a tree, with fierce eyes and a hooked beak. Its entire body was covered with purple and white shell *beads* instead of *feathers*. Alarmed by the girl's tale, the elders of the village decided that they must find the monster and determine what it was.

Going out to the marsh, the Wampum Bird was found feeding on the cranberries. The bird was not afraid of the humans and ran after them, sending them fleeing in fear! Several were wounded by the bird's attack and the men knew that obtaining the *wampum* it was made from would not be an easy task. It was promised that whoever killed the Wampum Bird would be given the beautiful daughter of the chief in marriage. However, after many tries, it seemed as if nothing could wound or kill the monster bird.

Finally, a young Delaware warrior came and slew the Wampum Bird, much to the surprise of all. The Iroquis acknowledged the Delaware as their kinsman and passed the wampum beads back and forth amongst themselves. From then on, the Delawares and the Iroquis lived in peace and no treaty was ever signed without the passing of a wampum belt made from the beads taken from the monster Wampum Bird.

Wankan-Tanka Wankan-Tanka was the Creator and Controller of the universe to the *Sioux* people, the Great Mystery, the *Great Spirit* that prevaded all things, including the Earth, *sun*, *moon*, stars, animals and humans.

Warm Springs See *Tribes*.

Washakie Washakie was of Umatilla and Flathead Indian blood. Born in 1804, at the age of 32 he joined the *Shoshone* tribe and quickly rose to power as their chief. The Shoshones called him 'White-Haired Chief with Scarred Face'. Washakie fought long and hard to defend his people against the *Crows*, *Sioux*, *Cheyennes* and Arapahoes. He also protected the whites against the Sioux and the Cheyennes.

Although the Shoshones were awarded a vast expanse of land when peace came, 15 years later the U.S. government announced that they would be moved to a reservation with the Arapahoes, their bitter enemies. Chief Washakie spoke out strongly against the move, reminding the government that he had never killed a white man, and his speeches spread his fame throughout Congress. He was assured that the move was just a temporary measure, but the Arapahoes moved in and are still there to this day.

Washakie died in 1900. He is buried at Fort Washakie, where some say *Sakajawea* is also buried.

Wasis See *Glooscap*.

Water Babies This term comes from a Paiute legend that centers around Pyramid Lake, Nevada. It is said that if you walk around the lake or on the bank of the Truckee River, you can see small tracks like a baby's. One time a man set a trap to catch an animal and instead caught a water baby. The next morning there was blood nearby and the steel trap was in little pieces—the water baby had broken out and escaped.

Water Indians See *Tribes*.

Water Serpent Ceremony The Water Serpent Ceremony is a *Hopi* ceremony called Palolokon by the tribe. It is not performed annually; dates are fixed according to Hopi secret tradition. It takes place inside the *kiva* where *corn* shoots are stuck in clay, representing a real cornfield. Huge horned *serpents* appear and, while the Mudheads sing (see *Hopi, Kachina*), they wipe away the little cornfield with violent gestures and motions. The Mother of All Kachinas approaches the serpents with a tray of cornmeal and 'nurses' each of them. The Mudheads then try to push the serpents back under *sun shields* which have been placed in the kiva, but the serpents resist. Finally, they are forced back and the shields are closed. The kiva is darkened for a short time and the performers depart.

It is said that this ceremony is given in honor of the giant reptiles who control the Earth's waters. Keeping these creatures happy helps to ensure the needed moisture for crops and to replenish the springs upon which the Indians depend.

Weaving Many Indian *tribes* are excellent weavers, particularly the *Navajo*. Navajo raise their own sheep and make their own looms and dye in order to produce beautiful rugs and *blankets* that have various geometric designs and often depict traditional scenes and *ceremonies*. Each area of the Navajo reservation has developed its own style of weaving: the Tuba City area is known for its 'storm' designs, which are jagged lightning symbols with a square symbol in the middle, while the Shiprock weavers usually weave the *Yei* design, that is, a design of tall figures that represent supernatural beings. The most common colors used in all rugs are gray, white, black and red.

The Navajo have been weavers for over 250 years, but the weaving of blankets is a dead art and the weaving of rugs is rapidly dying out. The scarcity of genuine Navajo rugs of fine quality is such that their value is rapidly increasing.

Whales Whales are sacred to the Indians of the Pacific northwest and Alaska. They are also a major source of *food*. The orca or killer whale is often depicted on *totem poles*. In *Eskimo* myths, whales were created from the frozen fingers of *Sedna*, the Sea Witch, which she lost trying to escape with her father from her husband, a storm petrel.

White Buffalo Woman It was the White Buffalo Woman who brought the gift of the sacred pipe to the *Sioux* people. She first appeared to the Sioux in human form. Before she came, the people did not know how to live. She taught them how to pray and the right words to speak and the right gestures. She also taught them the proper way to use the sacred pipe. As she walked off to the west, the direction from which she had come, she stopped and rolled over four times. Each time she turned into a *buffalo*—first a black one, then brown, then red and, finally, a white female buffalo calf. To this day, the Sioux consider the white buffalo to be the most sacred living thing that one can ever encounter.

White Deerskin Dance This *dance* is done by the Hupa Indians of northern California. It is unique in its costumes and form and perfectly captures the relationship of the people to their world. The dance also creates a ceremonial *language* that is only understood by the participants.

White Shell Man White Shell Man is the spirit of the *moon* to the *Navajo* Indians.

White Shell Woman Called Yolkai Estsan by the *Navajo*, White Shell Woman is the sister of *Changing Woman*, the Creator. Sometimes she is respected as another aspect of Changing Woman rather than as a separate deity. It was White Shell Woman who brought light to the Earth.

Wickiup The wickiup is a type of dwelling that was common to many of the eastern woodland Indian *tribes*. It is built by anchoring a framework of poles in the ground, bending them over and lashing them together to form a small dome. At this stage, the wickiup looks like a bare Sweat Lodge (see *Inipi*). Others poles can be added horizontally. The Indians who used this type of home laced on birchbark, but other materials may be used. A layer of plastic or canvas under the covering will keep things a lot cleaner inside.

Wigwam The wigwam is a style of Indian dwelling that was used long before the Europeans came. Said to be superior to the *tipi*, it was used by the people of the north central states and was a framework of any kind of sapling wood covered with tree bark. The *medicine* lodges of the Menomini Indians were built in the same manner. A smoke hole would be left in the wigwam roof, but it would be built so that it could be closed when desired. A fireplace was placed in the middle of the wigwam by setting stones halfway into the ground and then packing clay around the inside, against the stones, making a pan-shaped design. The fireplace was used for cooking during times of bad weather and the smoke also drove mosquitoes away in the summer.

Wilson, Jack See *Wovoka*.

Windigo Common to the *Chippewa* Indians, Windigos are fierce creatures made of stone and mud who are believed to be sorcerers with great powers. They are the enemies of the people and can freeze them into trances and hold them there indefinitely. They also eat people.

Winter Solstice The winter solstice, 21 December, was an important time for the Native Americans. It was a time for prayers and *ceremonies* to ensure the renewal of the Earth after the cold freezes of winter, and also a time to pray for the return of the *sun* in the spring. Some *tribes* sent prayers to the snow spirits so that they would come and bring moisture to make the rivers, streams and lakes full in the spring. People would also pray for protection from the cold, wind and blizzards of winter. To the *Hopi*, the winter solstice was the beginning of the new ceremonial year and the time for performing the *Soyal* Ceremony.

Wiwanyag Wachipi See *Sun Dance*.

Wolf Star The Wolf Star, believed to be the star Sirius, was sacred to the Wolf band of the *Pawnee* Indians. The star was said to be in the southeast and was connected with death.

Wood Fraternity See *Black Rock*.

Wounded Knee See *Ghost Dance*, *Wovoka*.

Wovoka Wovoka, a Paiute, was the son of an Indian prophet who was raised by a white couple by the name of Shures in Walker Lake, Nevada. He was given the name Jack Wilson. During an eclipse of the *sun*, Wovoka went into a trance and received a powerful vision. The trance was like a state of death and lasted for three days and three nights. When it was over, he returned to his people, and told them of his dream-vision.

Wovoka told his people that during his vision he had seen major changes coming, that there would be great shaking of the Earth and great storms. He said that a spirit would come to the Earth and raise all the dead, that the *buffalo* would return and that there would be an abundance of *food*, that there would be a great flood and the whites would leave their land forever. Wovoka said that the spirit was the 'Force' of the cosmos and that it had taught him a *dance*. If he would teach the dance to his people it would save them from defeat. His people should dance all day and all night until they also fell into a trance which would give them entrance into the 'ghost world'. While in trance they would receive visions that would help them to survive the difficult times. Wovoka was also told how to make a so-called 'ghost shirt' that would protect the wearer from death from the white man's bullets (see *Ghost Dance Shirt*). Most historians credit *Black Elk*, the Oglala *medicine man*, with designing and making the ghost shirts.

Wovoka gained permission from the *medicine* people to teach the dance to the people and it was embraced most ardently, especially by the Dakotas. Unfortunately, the whites saw it as a renewal of hostilities, realizing that it involved a magic that they could not control. Unaware of these fears, Indians would gather to perform the *Ghost Dance*, some coming from great distances. One such group, numbering some 300 women, children and old people, were on their way to a Ghost Dance in 1890 when they were slaughtered by Gatlin guns at Wounded Knee, South Dakota.

Wuwuchim Wuwuchim is one of the three winter *ceremonies* that begin the new ceremonial year for the *Hopi* and during which three phases of Creation are portrayed by the Wuchim Society and other participating societies. It is observed by certain villages on each of the mesas.

The ceremony re-enacts the first dawn of Creation, and is for the germination of all lifeforms on Earth, including plants, animals and man. It takes place in November, the actual date being determined by lunar observation. Beginning on the first day of the new *moon*, the participants gather the materials they will use to make *pahos* or prayer sticks. The pahos are made on the second day and prayed over on the third day. The following day they are carried to the proper shrines and the Public Crier announces the beginning of Wuwuchim from a rooftop.

The ceremony last for 16 days—half for preparation and half for secret rituals. On the day after the ceremony, there is a public dance. Wuwuchim also concludes the old year so it could be said that it both opens and closes the Hopi ceremonial cycle.

Y

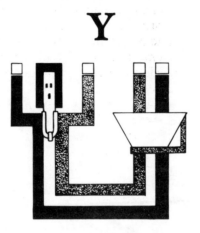

Yei, the Navajo Earth Spirit

Yakima See *Tribes*.

Yaqui The Yaqui are a tribe of southwestern Indians whose traditional religion has been greatly changed by Catholicism, which was brought by Jesuit priests in the early 1600s. The Yaqui were willing and enthusiastic converts and observe a full Roman Catholic ceremonial calendar. The rituals are led by Yaqui men who are called 'maestros' rather than Catholic priests. Yaqui churches are independent of the Roman Catholic Church. Their most elaborate *ceremonies* are those that have to do with their version of Lent and Easter. The Fariseo and Caballero Societies are in charge of these ceremonies.

Yehwehnode See *Twylah Nitsch*.

Yei A Yei is a *Navajo* deity, the Earth Spirit.

Yei-bi-chai Yei-bi-chai, also known as the Navajo Night Chant, is a *dance* in which the cosmic world of the Navajo is made visible and real through ceremony. It is a night dance held around bonfires and accompanied by mysterious *chants*. The ceremonials begin at sundown and end eight and a half days later at sunrise. The first four days are devoted to purification for the Yei-bi-chai is also a *healing* dance.

Yolkai Estsan See *White Shell Woman*.

Yuwipi Yuwipi is one of the most ancient rites of the *Sioux* Indians. As revealed by *John Fire Lame Deer*, the term 'yuwipi' has many meanings. However, it is usually used to indicate small shiny rocks that are picked up at anthills and considered to be sacred and extremely powerful by the Sioux. Four hundred and five of these rocks are placed inside *gourds* that are used in *ceremonies*, the number corresponding to the number of trees in Sioux country. The power of these sacred rocks is called 'yuwipi wasicun', which is also another name for Tunka, the most ancient of all Sioux gods, who, like a rock, is ageless and eternal. Rocks have always been special to the Indians and are often used, as with the Sioux, in *healing* ceremonies.

In the Yuwipi Ceremony, the spirits and lights which dwell in the sacred stones talk to a *medicine man* who has placed a twig of sagebrush behind his ear so that he will understand their message. The Yuwipi Ceremony is held when a person needs help to find something lost or stolen. The person must first send a peace pipe to a yuwipi medicine man. Not all medicine men practice yuwipi. There is no fee for the medicine man's services but the sponsor must provide *food* for all who participate and attend the ceremony. The Yuwipi Ceremony also requires a young dog, who is marked with red paint and strangled. A woman then singes off its hair, cuts it up and boils it, for its meat is essential to the ceremony. The dog is sacrificed so that the people might live. His meat helps to cure the sick and gives them strength.

In the room where the Yuwipi Ceremony is to take place, no light is allowed to enter. It is held at night, and even the glow of the *moon* is not allowed to interrupt the blackness. The floor is covered with sagebrush, which represents the powers of Nature. Four hundred and five *tobacco* ties, made by the women, are tied onto a string and formed into a rectangle on the floor, leaving just enough room between the rectangle and the wall for people to sit down with their legs outstretched. The interior of the rectangle is sacred. Four 'flags' are placed at the four corners of the rectangle: red for the north and the pipestone, yellow for the east and the rising *sun*, black for the west and darkness, and white for the south and the sun at its zenith. Between the black and red flags, there is a stick that is half red and half black, with a thin white stripe separating the two. The red is for day and the black for night. The stick is topped with an *eagle* feather which represents the power from above. The spotted eagle is the wisest of all living creatures to the Sioux. Halfway down the stick hangs the tail of a special kind of *deer* with a black streak across its face. The deer is also sacred, and represents the unity of the universe. The five sticks, which are made of special skunkwood branches, are planted in cans filled with sand. An altar is built behind the red and black center stick, made from powdered earth made smooth with an eagle feather. Through this altar, the whole Earth is present during the ceremony. A design is traced in the altar by the medicine man, one that is sacred to the yuwipi *shaman* and embodies a particular magic. *Rattles* are also used in the ceremony and, as a rule, there are two of them, although some medicine men use four, one for each direction. The rattles are believed to speak to the people. The pipe is also involved.

The pot of dog meat and another filled with water from a spring are placed inside the rectangle, near the red flag. Other foods, that will be distributed after the ceremony, are placed outside the rectangle.

Before the ceremony actually begins, the room and all the sacred objects are purified with sweetgrass smoke (see also *Smudging*). A bag of 'Indian perfume' is passed around and each person rubs it on their bodies and clothing so that they will smell like Nature. No one is allowed inside the rectangle but the yuwipi medicine man. As the ceremony begins, he stands before the altar ready to be tied up with rawhide, starting with the fingers, which are tied to each other with the arms behind the back. The medicine man is then completely wrapped up in a *buffalo* hide or a blanket that has the design of the morning star on it. Next, the man and the blanket are tied tightly into a bundle so that he will feel the pain of the people and so that the spirits can come to him and use him. He is then taken and placed with his head near the altar and lies there as if dead.

Sacred songs and prayers ensue. The spirits come from the west and the south in the form of sparks of light. They are everywhere, above and below, causing the walls and the floor to tremble. They also come as little voices which can be heard and understood.

The ceremony lasts for a long time. When it is over and the lights are turned on, the medicine man is found sitting unwrapped and untied with the tobacco ties around him. He allows the people to ask questions of him and will answer them—if he has received the power while wrapped up. He lights the sacred pipe and it is passed around among the people. A little of the dog meat is then eaten by the sick. A young boy comes around the room with water and the people drink the youth-restoring liquid. Without further activities or words, the people then leave, the ceremony completed.

Z

Zuni Polychrome Ceramic Vessel

Zia The Zia is the symbol of the *sun* to the *Zuni* people, and they live on the Zia *pueblo* in the Rio Grande valley, New Mexico, one of four pueblo groups that are divided linguistically. The people there perform the same *ceremonies* as the other pueblos, however, in spite of the language difference.

Zuni The Zuni *pueblo* is located 40 miles south of Gallup, New Mexico, in Valencia County. It is the only surviving pueblo of Coronado's fabled Seven Cities of Cibola, and is the largest pueblo in New Mexico. It was once the center of a large number of settlements and in the early days the entire region was the scene of incomparable pageantry and drama. The Indians called the land 'Shivona'. An advance party of Spaniards arrived in the area in 1539 and found the Zunis, who by that time had been there for over 500 years. Later, after the whites came to the Rio Grande, the tribe roamed eastward and north to the Gila River.

The Zuni pueblo is still occupied today and the people there continue to perform their *ceremonies*, some of which are open to the public.

Zuni Neweekee Known as the Galaxy Fraternity, the Zuni

Neweekee is a secret society of *shamans* who seek to heal the sick by the use of magic and invocation. Its members are required to pass difficult, bizarre tests such as the eating of human excrement.

Bibliography

Brown, John Eppes, *The Sacred Pipe: Black Elk's Account of the Seen Sacred Rites of the Sioux*, Penguin Books, London, 1971.

Brown, Vinson, *Voices of Earth and Sky*, Naturegraph Publishers, Inc, Happycamp, California, 1974.

Chamberlain, Von Del, *When Stars Came Down to Earth: The Cosmology of the Skidi Pawnee Indians of North America*, Ballena Press, Center for Archeoastronomy Cooperation Publication, Los Altos, California, 1982.

Curtis, Edward S., *In a Sacred Manner We Live*, Weathervane Books, New York, 1972.

Erdoes, Richard, and Ortiz, Alfonso, *American Indian Myths and Legends*, Pantheon Fairy Tale and Folklore Library, Pantheon Books, New York, 1984.

Fergusson, Erna, *Dancing Gods: Indian Ceremonials of New Mexico and Arizona*, University of New Mexico Press, Albuquerque, New Mexico, 1931.

Gifford, Barry (ed.), *The Portable Curtis: Selected Writings of Edward S. Curtis*, Creative Arts Book Company, Berkeley, California, 1976.

Haddington, Evan, *Early Man and the Cosmos*, University of Oklahoma Press, Norman, Oklahoma, 1989.

Hoffman, John F., *Grand Canyon Visual*, Western Recreational Publications, San Diego, California, 1987.

Howard, Helen Addison, *Saga of Chief Joseph*, University of Nebraska Press, Lincoln, Nebraska, and London, 1965.

Hunt, Ben W., *The Complete How-To Book of Indian Crafts*, Collier Books, New York, 1973.

Locke, Raymond Friday, *The Book of the Navajo*, Mankind House Publishing Company, Los Angeles, California, 1976.

Marquis, Arnold, *A Guide to America's Indians*, University of Oklahoma Press, Norman, Oklahoma, 1960.

Right, Barton V., *Kachinas: A Hopi Artist's Documentary*, Northland Press, Flagstaff, Arizona, 1973.

Southwestern Indian Ceremonials, 170 KC Publications, Inc, revision by Mark Bahti, Las Vegas, Nevada, 1982.

Sun Bear, *Buffalo Hearts*, Bear Tribe Publishing Company, Spokane, Washington, 1970.

Sun Bear, and Wabun, *Self-Reliance Book*, Nimimosha and The Bear Tribe Medicine Society, Bear Tribe Publishing Company, Spokane, Washington, 1980.

Tanner, Clara Lee, *Hopi Kachinas*, Ray Manley Publishing, Tucson, Arizona.

Wabun with Weinstock, Barry, *Sun Bear: The Path of Power*, Bear Tribe Publishing Company, Spokane, Washington, 1983.

Waters, Frank, *Book of the Hopi*, Penguin Books, 1972.

Weltfish, Gene, *The Lost Universe: Pawnee Life and Culture*, University of Nebraska Press, Lincoln, Nebraska, 1977.

Wood, Marion, *Spirits, Heroes and Hunters from North American Indian Mythology*, Schocken Books, New York, 1981.

The Aquarian Guide to African Mythology

Jan Knappert

Africa: the most distinctive land mass on the surface of the earth. Yet for all its majesty it is a country whose historical and religious wealth remains a mystery to all but a very few of Western observers. How many people know anything at all about pre-Colonial Africa?

The Aquarian Guide to African Mythology is the first comprehensive overview of the beliefs, myths and cosmology of African peoples. It deals not only with traditional stories woven around a pantheon of gods and mythical figures but also with legends, fables and more general subjects that played a part in African mythology and African life. The wide range of entries include religious concepts, prophets, the best-known tribes, mystical phenomena, spirits and demons, and the many animals that played such a large part in African mythology.

Dr Jan Knappert's alphabetical guide is founded on his many years of personal experience in Africa. Its very accessible style makes it ideal not only as a reference work for students of anthropology but as a sample for general readers wishing to dip in and be informed on any subject that appeals to them. The book is fully cross-referenced and is illustrated with examples of African art. Wherever the reader opens it, he or she will be informed, stimulated to further thought and study, and entertained.

The Aquarian Guide to Greek Mythology

Richard Stoneman

Zeus and Athena, Heracles and Achilles, Delphi and Olympia, Medusa and the Minotaur . . . the stuff of the oldest and most powerful mythological tradition in Europe. As familiar to most people as the characters and events in the Bible, the great legendary heroes and stories of classical Greece are a unique legacy, their traditions having influenced the art, literature and culture of Western Europe like no other. Yet for all the colourful sources that exist — from Homer downwards — it is still difficult for the enthusiast to piece together a coherent picture of the genuine uncorrupted traditions of Greek mythology.

The Aquarian Guide to Greek Mythology is the key to the jigsaw. Including in dictionary form all the major figures of Greek mythology, the book provides a handy but comprehensive guide for newcomers and offers further help to those who want to learn more. Deliberately excluding the Roman myths which can blur the true image of the Greek heritage, Richard Stoneman covers the gods, heroes and men, places, mythical creatures and religious terminology that make up the whole gamut of Greek mythology. Complete with illustrations based on contemporary Greek art, the book is also the first to encompass both classical and post-classical folklore and legend, bringing in Alexander the Great, vampires and the terrible kallikantzaroi, which will broaden the vocabulary of all who are interested in the wealth that is Greek mythology.